PRAISE FOR
WE tv's
THE LOCATOR

"…'The Locator'…is worth a look, let me tell you."
—Dr. Phil

"The Locator' always delivers…it's reliably, and honestly, moving…"
—New York Times

"..there's no denying he's the best in the business…"
—Star Magazine

"…feels a lot more 'real' than almost any other 'reality' program out there."
—NY Daily News

"In a sea of exploitative or pointless reality entertainment, *The Locator* is a shining light of positivity that deserves to be found"
—TV Squad

IT'S NEVER TOO LATE:
LESSONS FOR LIFE FROM
THE LOCATOR

TROY DUNN

AYLESBURY
PUBLISHING

To my eternal companion Jennifer, our 7 extraordinary children and to Mom and Dad. These 10 indivduals are directly responsible for my joy, success and dreams.
I LOVE YOU ETERNALLY.

CONTENTS

INTRODUCTION

Now in its fifth season, WE tv's *The Locator* seems to have found a place in the hearts of its viewers, people who share the joys of our successful reunions and the sadness when a longed-for reunion doesn't take place. You, our audience, have become a cheering section for the communion and sense of peace that reunions can bring, and we thank you very much for your enthusiasm and support. We very much appreciate your endorsement of our life's work. I also believe the extraordinary success of *The Locator* is compelling proof that the family unit is still the backbone of the world we live in. To most people, family is all. In loving families, people find the strength and support they need to move forward with their lives. Watching *The Locator* allows our audience to root for others seeking to reconnect to the deep bonds that unite families, and in watching successful reunions take place, we all somehow become better people, sharing the deep satisfaction, joy and healing that loving families create.

I know this now, but five years ago, I have to admit that agreeing to be a part of "The Locator" was not a decision I arrived at easily. I had been reuniting families for over 20 years, but our reunions were usually very private matters, handled delicately with phone calls, and quiet meetings in people's homes where hugs and healing took place among a small group of family members. There was no audience, no television cameras or sound technicians recording these often highly emotional reunions. So when I was approached with the idea of opening up the search journey for others to experience, I wasn't at all sure that sharing these private moments with millions of people was a good idea, and said so to my colleagues. However, during a long conversation with my mother, she said something that really struck a chord with me.

"Perhaps we will be able to inspire other families to take the journey we know to be so healing. Troy, we have an opportunity to share what we love so much with so many. How can we not?"

That was the day I agreed to participate in *The Locator*. She turned about to be absolutely right, of course, as only mothers can be, and five seasons later, I have never regretted our decision.

Being *The Locator* has made me a crusader of sorts as well, a cheerleader for the human spirit, as I meet so many brave people who trust me enough to risk potential rejection or heartbreak in order to reunite with a loved one. I am inspired by how tenaciously they persevere in hopes of finding a missing person from their lives, how sturdily they weather the emotional ups and downs that are part of their quests, and I watch them change right before my eyes as they embrace the peace they have found. Witnessing this extraordinary combination of courage and hope in so many hundreds of people has taught me more about the goodness of life than I could ever otherwise hope to know.

But being a part of so many powerful personal journeys has also led me to my own inward journey. How is it that I have been so blessed to have found my life's work as *The Locator*?

I was drawn to reunions when, as most viewers know, I was able to find my own mother's birth mother. That reunion ended unhappily as my biological grandmother refused to acknowledge my mother, a hurt I know Mom still carries. But in that first search I learned that I had a gift for perseverance and that helping my mother find and face her past was very important and very rewarding for me.

But reflecting further back in my life, I began to realize, in hindsight, that there were earlier signs that reuniting loved ones would become my eventual career.

My family moved a lot when I was young. A lot. I went to a different school every year from kindergarten to my freshman year in high school. I was always the "new kid." Luckily, I was good at making friends so I fit in pretty quickly in each new school. But then, at the end of each school year, we moved again, and I had to say goodbye to another set of friends I'd hoped would be a continuing part of my life. Throughout my childhood I was in an almost constant state of missing someone. I now see that part of my determination to reunite people as *The Locator* comes from the long trail of people who came and went in my own life and my yearning to see them again.

That this was so became very apparent last year when, for a case for *The Locator*, I had to fly to Anchorage, Alaska.

One of the toughest years for our family was when I was in sixth grade and we lived in Alaska. Despite my Dad's heroic efforts to provide for our family, we struggled financially. At one point, we couldn't even pay the rent for our house, and so, with great pain, Dad moved us into a campground for a short period of time, where we lived in a friend's little RV. My younger siblings saw it as an extended camping trip and probably loved it, but I was old enough to know what was really going on and was very sad for my Mom and Dad. Nobody at school knew our shaky circumstances nor did I share them with my friends. The only person to whom I even hinted my worries was my teacher, Mrs. Barter. She sensed my troubles and somehow knew just when to give me a reassuring hug and provide a comforting voice to ease tough days. She showed me great kindness at a time when hope was in short supply.

But that memory was locked away in the back of my brain until the day we flew into Anchorage. That morning, I was idly staring out the window of the plane, looking down on the city, when I was suddenly overwhelmed by vivid memories of my difficult year there and by all the emotions that had accompanied my experiences. In the midst of many painful recollections I remembered how important Mrs. Barter had been to me then and realized I owed her a great deal. I wondered if she was still around, still teaching and if she would remember me. I'm *The Locator*, I suddenly thought. Why not use my skills for my own reunion?

As soon as we got on the ground, I grabbed my rental car, and while the crew went for lunch, I shifted into full Locator mindset and began tracing Mrs. Barter's steps. I called the local school board and my own old school and found that she was still in Anchorage, teaching at another school, and I quickly drove there.

As I walked into the building and got closer to the school office, I felt like I was eleven years old again. The quiet confidence that I rely upon to help my clients deal with their fears completely disappeared and I was suddenly filled with anxiety. My heart was pounding and I could barely breathe. I was behaving exactly like the many people I work with on *The Locator* when they are on the cusp of a reunion, only this time it was me!

A woman from the school office took me down the hall toward Mrs. Barter's classroom. She seemed surprised when I told her I was a former student, probably because I looked to be the same age as Mrs. Barter. I would later learn that the year Mrs. Barter was my teacher was her first as a teacher. Here I was, one of her first students, striding nervously toward her classroom as she was in the twilight of her long teaching career.

I would be lying if I didn't confess to second-guessing my decision with every step. It wasn't that I felt I was doing the wrong thing, but I was unsure of what I would say and worse, was afraid that she wouldn't remember me. I knew that would be devastating to me, even as an adult.

As we stepped into the doorway of the classroom, there she was across the room, sitting at her desk talking to a student. I couldn't hear what was being said, but imagined that he was another lucky child benefiting from the wise and loving counsel of my cherished teacher.

My heart was leaping out of my chest, but I forced myself to smile as the woman I was with motioned for Mrs. Barter. She started towards me with a sober but questioning expression on her face. As she got within a few steps she said, "Troy?"

I couldn't believe it! She had seen through my middle age to the eleven-year-old boy who had been so grateful for her attention. I gave her a hug that I'm sure lingered longer than she expected, but it couldn't have lasted long enough for me.

In that moment, I found a whole new level of conviction to my life's work. You really can't find peace until you find all the pieces. I didn't even know I had a piece missing from that long ago chapter of my life, but seeing Mrs. Barter that day seemed to be the realization that we (as a family) had made it. We are good. We survived a difficult journey and the sun still shines, Alaska is still beautiful and Mrs. Barter is still..... Mrs. Barter!

The deep fulfillment I feel in arranging reunions drives me to work hard to make them happen, but yearning alone is not enough to bring people together. To succeed in the way I have, you need determination, resilience and perseverance. For those skills, I thank my experience as a high school and college football player.

I have always loved football, but as I get older, I realize that it has had a huge impact on my life. Like many former child-athletes, I trace many of my life skills to what I learned in those intense years of competition, both the victories and the defeats, when I played fullback for Enid High School. Two philosophies in particular that I took from the football field to the business of being *The Locator* are to never quit and to recognize the importance of a team.

From time to time, while working on a challenging case, the kind of case that keeps me up at night because I want so desperately to grant this wish, fix this broken heart, stop somebody's suffering, and all of the other weighty issues people attach to their searches, and which put a lot of pressure to bear upon me and the team, I think I'm at a dead end. We've followed up every possible lead, from relatives to government offices, public registries of all kinds, the internet, even the telephone book and have come up empty. I am very discouraged and have the horrible feeling that we're going to have to tell our client we can't help him.

It is then that I find myself motivated, even haunted, by the voices of football coaches past. They urge me on, reminding me that winners never quit and quitters never win, shouting that anything worth having comes with sacrifice, and all of the other heart-pounding, mind-shifting statements that they instilled in me through repetition. This disciplined training, drummed into me on the gridiron, calls me back to action, and we redouble our efforts to solve a case. And, while we may not always find who we are looking for, we are always striving for victory.

As important as true grit is to building a good team, football taught me that you don't have to be good at everything. But everybody is good at something, and if you find the right people and unite them behind a shared vision, you can fight together for a team victory. The first team member I recruited into my life's work was my mother, and she continues to be our star and leading scorer. Through her passion and commitment, I was able to attract other skilled, talented people to round out the team. I have never, never considered myself the star of the team, but rather the coach. I seek talented folks and then do my best to design a game plan that will maximize their skill set and bring about victory. For us, every reunion is a win. Like all teams, we don't win them all, but we learn from our losses, put them aside and start prepping for the next game!

Finally, I think that a very traumatic family experience was the catalyst for my work today on television. I started my original locating business in 1990 and over the next twelve years, built it into a very successful company. We helped thousands of people find loved ones and experienced all the emotions of crying, hugging, celebrating and mourning with our clients. But, by the end of that time, I was completely drained and exhausted by the emotional demands of the work, and sadly, came to the conclusion that I could no longer be effective as a *locator*. So I sold the company to *Ancestry.com* and began my gradual separation from the work I'd loved for so long.

Then one of the most terrifying things that can happen to a family happened to us. Our daughter, Josalin, then seven years old, was diagnosed with cancer, and our world came to a screeching halt. We rallied around her and her medical care became my fulltime job and obsession. Many nights were spent in various hospitals and Ronald McDonald Houses around the country as we worked to cure our little girl. That year I believed I would never reunite another family again.

But adversity is meant to be temporary, despite how it feels at the time, and when it passed and Josalin was one of the lucky ones—she has now been clean for five years—I felt a new energy and commitment to families and to the peace that reunions can bring. It was at that time that we were asked about a television show. Realizing how I missed the work I loved and deciding that we could continue to help people by reaching a large audience who would see the blessings that come from renewing ties with loved ones, we agreed to go forward. *The Locator*, was born.

When I see the arc of my life and how I was led to the work I do, I feel an enormous gratitude for the opportunities I've been given and a determination to help as many people as I can to feel the peace and fulfillment that come with connecting with loved ones.

And that brings us to this book. My journey as "The Locator" has enriched my life and armed me with powerful life-building tools that I find myself driven to share. I truly believe reading this book can help everyone lead better, richer lives. I have combed through my notes and memories for the hundreds of inspiring words, brave decisions made in the face of fear, acts of stunning forgiveness and the wonderful shouts of happiness that I have witnessed in my work. I have organized them into eleven insights that can help you slowly and steadily transform your own lives for the better.

When you read these truths, you will see that each asks you, in different ways, to shift from hopelessness to hope, from inaction to action, from negative to positive.

They require effort and you may get stuck thinking you're incapable of forgiveness, or would rather walk away from a situation rather than do the work to repair a relationship. But if this happens, I urge you to think of the people who appear on *The Locator* or even download a few shows and watch them again. You will see that each of my clients chose to listen to their deepest wishes and asked us to help them take a journey to the unknown. For some there is a happy ending, for others disappointment, but in taking action, they embraced their lives fully and with hope. I promise you that you can do the same.

Enjoy the journey and see you on *The Locator*.

CHAPTER 1

Time Does Not
Heal All Wounds

One thing I've learned as WE tv's *The Locator* is that time has been way oversold as a fixer.

In my work, I've seen people who, for seemingly logical reasons, wait years and years before seeking out loved ones. They often can't find someone without professional help. Fear of rejection is another big reason why someone waits for decades to begin a search for a missing loved one. Who wants to get hurt twice? Personal problems like alcohol or drug abuse also keep people from beginning a search for a lost relative or friend.

But even the people with good reasons for delay almost always, when they experience the joy and wonderful sense of completion a reunion brings, voice regret for the time they've missed being together.

"Why did I wait so long?" is one of the most common laments I hear from people who have finally found a loved one.

Donna Gardner, sixty-one, was someone who waited almost a lifetime before being reunited with a daughter she had given up for adoption when she was nineteen. At the time, she was unmarried, unemployed and an alcoholic and knew she was doing the right thing in arranging for her daughter to have a stable home and a caring environment that she could not provide. But even after changing her life—becoming clean, and starting a successful career as a drug and alcohol counselor to help those who had suffered as she had--she was haunted by her loss. Finally her niece contacted us from Sacramento, California, for help.

"She went down the wrong path, but she rose above it, and even though she's done all these good things to make up for the bad, she's still not happy. I want her to know that she is a mother even though she doesn't have a child," Stephanie told me when I visited her and Donna at their home.

For more than forty years Donna said, "I had a hole in my heart." She hoped that her daughter was loved and taken care of in her adoptive home, and missed her terribly. But she was reluctant to look for her, fearing her daughter's anger and rejection.

To add to her pain, one day she got a call from a young woman who thought she was Donna's daughter, and Donna was thrilled, hoping to finally meet the person she had given away as a baby. But after talking and sharing their stories, the women realized that there had been a mistake.

"'The county has made a mistake, but you will always be my mother,' she told me," Donna said to me, "but she never called again."

This sad trick of fate devastated Donna. She thought she would never get a chance to connect with her own child.

Finally, her niece persuaded her to contact me. My team was able to find Gail Harris Mims, who lives in San Jose, California, with her husband and three children. She was eager to meet her birth mother. For years she had wondered why her mother had given her up for adoption and had, in fact, considered contacting *The Locator* herself a year earlier.

But she told me, "I was afraid of being rejected," so she had done nothing.

We arranged a reunion for the two women, who, far from turning away from each other, were thrilled to meet. Gail enveloped her mother in a warm embrace, and the two women, crying and holding on to each other, began to share their lives. Donna felt relieved that her daughter was happy and healthy and Gail was very grateful for her mother's unselfishness in giving her up to be raised in a stable home.

Seeing this mother and daughter discover how much they loved each after a lifetime apart, watching their eagerness to touch, learn about each other and commit themselves to a future together was to see very clearly how time had cheated them.

The very moment Donna's 41-year search for her daughter, Gail, comes to an emotional close.

Time also played too large a part in the many years that a Houston man spent yearning to meet his older brother. Ricardo's mother, Kelly, had given her firstborn son up for adoption before Ricardo was born, and had told Ricardo, when he was seven years old, that he had a half brother. An only child, Ricardo had wanted to meet his brother ever since and now, finally, with his mother's approval, had contacted us for help.

4

Kelly had been a twenty-year-old college student when she became pregnant during a brief affair. In 1969, it was hard for her to imagine how she could raise a baby on her own.

"Then you had to be in a family, and I couldn't offer that. I didn't know what to do," she said.

She decided that giving up the baby was the best option for him.

"I didn't know if it was better or not, but it was the decision I made and I had to live with it," she told me when we met at her home.

When Ricardo reached adulthood, he began to better understand how his mother had wrestled with her decision to give up her son, and how that might have made her feel too guilty to try to reconnect with him.

"Having children of my own, I can empathize with what it must have been like to have the ability to sacrifice your feelings for the good of the child," he said. "I want her to be able to know that she did the right thing."

I agreed to try to help Ricardo and Kelly find the son she'd named Christopher. His adopted parents had changed his first name, however, which made our search more difficult, but we finally located him in San Jose, California, where he worked as a flight engineer for the U.S. Air Force, rescuing soldiers by helicopter. He has served in both Iraq and Afghanistan and was married with five children. The baby Kelly had relinquished so many years earlier had grown up to be a living hero.

I met Christopher, now named Brock Walker, at his air

base, and he began to cry when he learned that his half brother and mother were looking for him.

After locating Brock, we sat down to discuss his hopes and fears about reuniting with his biological family.

He was raised in a very loving family with two siblings, both of whom had died, and was thrilled to hear that he had a younger brother. Brock agreed to fly to Houston with me to meet his birth family.

The reunion between mother and son, and brother and brother was heartfelt and joyous.

Kelly was so happy to know that Brock had grown up in a loving home. She was very excited to have both her sons with her, and both men were thrilled to have found a new brother.

"I can't explain to you what it's like, because for so many years we've had this kind of blank silhouette of who you would be when we finally met you, so to have you standing here—it's like almost overwhelming," Ricardo told Brock.

"And I've always wondered how my life would have been different if my Mom had kept me," Brock told him.

Now these men don't have to wonder any more.

Kelly finally has "baby boy" Brock back in her arms after 39 years.

I've watched many reunions that could have taken place much earlier if people had not believed that doing nothing was safer and better than searching for long-lost loved ones. They tried to tell themselves that time would heal them and make their pain and unhappiness disappear.

Time can do many things, but one thing it cannot do is repair wounds of the heart. In fact, time not only doesn't heal deep rifts and misunderstandings that come between loved ones; the more time that passes, the more those initial feelings can deepen and harden into negative beliefs. Precious years of joy and communion can be wasted by holding onto old misunderstandings and fears.

Every week I see what happens when walls are broken down and people allow themselves to love each other again. Years of anger and sadness seem to melt away, replaced by unbelievable acts of forgiveness, kindness and generosity. It is a great privilege to witness these moments of communion that are so full of love that it seems to spill over into our own hearts. I always return home with an even deeper gratitude for my own family after a successful reunion, determined to honor our love for one another.

My good fortune in seeing the human spirit blossom right before my eyes has filled me with a tremendous sense of urgency to help others know what my clients have learned, that spending time waiting to reconnect with loved ones is time wasted.

The clients on *The Locator* have carried their emotional burdens for years as a result of the forced absence of a loved one, but their suffering is not so different from that of unhappy family members living side by side who deeply hurt each other, hoping that time will somehow ease their pain.

In an odd way, in fact, my clients' situations are less complicated, because their alienation is as physical as it is emotional—they haven't been able to even try to repair their relationships because they simply can't find each other. But an unhappy couple facing each other across the dinner table confront their emotional separation every night. An offhand remark, an icy stare, or charged silences are frequent reminders that two people once in love have lost their connection to each other.

Time, far from healing them, becomes their enemy. Every day brings another opportunity to inflict or receive hurt and to justify feelings of rejection. They become more comfortable with their anger and suffering then they are in their love for each other. Walls are slowly built up between them, and then they begin to rearrange their relationship around these new barriers. Each starts to act like someone with a bad back who gets a spasm every time he bends down to tie his shoes. Rather than go to the doctor to get his back fixed, he starts wearing loafers. Pretty soon he gets so used to the loafers that the shoes he really prefers, the ones that are the most comfortable and stylish, are left sitting on the floor in the back of the closet.

The idea that people get mad at each other and stay that way for years isn't exactly breaking news. If we haven't looked in the mirror and acknowledged that we're guilty of holding a grudge against someone we love, we've seen it all around us among husbands, wives, sons, daughters, aunts and uncles and close friends.

Breaking long-standing patterns is never easy. Even the most destructive behavior becomes familiar, often comfortable after years of practice, and it takes a lot of courage to change the rules and reach out to someone who has hurt you deeply.

But the reunions I've helped arrange have taught me that people are stronger, more resilient and more forgiving than they might think. I can see that the payoffs for taking a chance can be life-changing for both the seeker and the person they find.

If you decide it's time to take a new look at some of your own relationships, but are afraid of what might happen, remember the courage of my clients on *The Locator*. Each of them took an incredible risk to try improve his or her life. Some succeeded beyond their wildest dreams in finding the happiness they sought. Others were sadly disappointed. But all were motivated by the realization that time wasn't going to change their circumstances. They had to take the first step themselves. Most would say they wished they done it sooner. But you don't have to wait. You can start right now.

CHAPTER 2

The Raw Power of Hugs

B efore I became WE tv's *The Locator*, hugging was not my greeting of choice. I shook hands, high-fived, maybe kissed someone on the cheek, but hugging? No. However, if there's one gesture I've learned to appreciate and celebrate after twenty years of helping people find loved ones, it's a warm, enveloping hug.

In my work, it's very important to both listen carefully to what clients tell me and to look at them with my full attention when we are together. Their words, obviously, give me the information I need to help them, but so do their eyes, their physical movements and their facial expressions—the latter reveal the emotions that underlie what they're telling me and give me important clues on how to proceed. A young man can say he's willing to meet a birth father who wants to reunite, but if he's tapping his hand on his thigh while he's talking and he's avoiding eye contact, I know that I have to slow things down, that he's not quite ready for a meeting. I believe that one of the reasons we've had such success on *The Locator* in guiding people toward happy reunions is in realizing that non-verbal clues are as important as conversation in ensuring that people are ready to embrace life-changing encounters.

So it's ironic that someone who respects the great power of non-verbal communication as I do was so clueless about hugs. I'd been arranging reunions for a long time before I began to notice that the physical act of hugging was key to a successful reunion.

Time after time, I would reintroduce loved ones who hadn't seen or heard from each other for years. In many ways they were complete strangers.

Yet when seeing each other for the first time after so long, what didn't they do? They didn't politely shake hands, or kiss on the cheek or touch each other's shoulder. Instead, at the best reunions, they fell into each other arms like soldiers home from war and they wouldn't let go.

They often cried. And then they hugged each other again. And then they would laugh and hug again—and again and again. The hugs were spontaneous and filled the rooms with what felt like balloons of happiness and healing.

The result of these frequent, warm embraces was that my tv crew had to learn to adjust for hugs. Everyone appearing on the show wears a small microphone, usually attached to their shirts or blouses, but when the hugs begin, the microphones are almost always pushed out of place by the power of peoples' embraces. So the audio crew now knows that when reunions take place, they need to have, at the ready, the long-distance boom microphone, which can be placed unobtrusively over peoples' heads to record conversations when the smaller microphones fail.

What is it about the power of hugs?

I believe that hugs communicate deep feelings when words don't come easily. When you open your arms and pull someone into a close embrace, you are going heart-to-heart in a very physical way, telling someone wordlessly that you are willing to move forward, perhaps one step at a time, to restart a relationship. Hugs are brave and powerful and show the human spirit at its most vulnerable and most generous.

On our show, hugs can mean many different things when two people reunite, from "I'm sorry," to "Thank you," to "I Love you." Often a hug means all three.

Mary Radcliffe and her husband, Clement, had taken care of their beloved foster daughter, Tamisha, for five years when the local child services agency abruptly took her away and put her up for adoption. Mary had no time to explain to the then-seven-year-old girl what was happening or even to explore adopting her herself. As devastated as she was to lose the little girl she loved, she was even more haunted by what had happened to Tamisha. So, twenty-five years after they were separated, Mary contacted me to find her foster daughter.

We were able to locate Tamisha, a single mother who lives in Queens, New York. She agreed instantly to meet Mary, so we flew together to Greensboro, North Carolina, to surprise Mary and her family, who were having lunch at a local restaurant.

When Tamisha walked into the dining room, Mary rose from her chair and moved toward her as if on autopilot, throwing her arms around her and pulling her into a vice-like embrace as if she never wanted to let her go. The only sound in the room was Mary's low cries of joy at seeing Tamisha again.

As I prepare Tamisha to meet her foster mom,
she can hardly contain her excitement!

It wasn't until Tamisha had hugged her foster sister, her foster aunt, Clement and Mary once more that Mary started trying to explain things, repeating over and over how sorry she was that Tamisha had been so cruelly removed from her home.

But by that time, the hugs had done their job. Tamisha knew from Mary's healing embrace how much she regretted losing her foster daughter, and Tamisha, in hugging her back, forgave her. There were no words. There didn't have to be.

On another case, a man named John Keuerleber showed me very clearly when a hug is better than words in communicating with someone you love.

Eighteen-year-old Alexia Keuerleber, a recent high school graduate, wanted to find her father. She hardly remembered him and only knew what her mother had told her about him, which was that he wasn't a nice guy. She was determined to find out for herself what kind of a man he was and to ask him why he'd disappeared from her life.

We did locate her father, John, a butcher from Campbell Hall, New York, who told us his side of the story. He and Alexia's mother had divorced, and while he had joint custody of his daughter, his ex-wife made his visits so difficult and uncomfortable, upsetting Alexia so much that he eventually stopped seeing her. Presents both he and his sisters sent to Alexia were returned and he had lost contact with her.

When I asked him what he would say to her if he were to meet her again after thirteen years, he told me, "I don't want to say anything. I just want to grab her and give her a big bear hug."

Which is exactly what he did when we arranged a reunion for them last year at an art gallery in Pennsylvania. He walked across the long room to greet her, and then, without speaking, just lifted her into the air and held her for what seemed like forever, rocking her back and forth as if she was the little five-year-old girl she'd been when they last saw each other. Alexia, tears streaming down her face as she hugged him back, knew then that he was never going to let her go again.

Who needs words when a loving embrace says everything?

One of my favorite moments ever—John literally sweeps his daughter Alexia off her feet!

I think one of my favorite hugs was between a long-separated father and son, Donald and Jeremy Burgess. Jeremy, thirty-seven, a single dad to two daughters who lived outside of Sacramento, California, yearned to find the father he'd never known. He'd been actively searching for him for more than fifteen years but had come up with nothing, so he contacted *The Locator* for help.

Talking with Donnie, I could see he ached for the son he was separated from decades earlier, but feared that myths about him may have been told to Jeremy.

Jeremy's parents had separated when he was a baby, and he was very confused by the answers to the questions he asked his mother, grandmother and aunt about his father. His mother and grandmother both said the man was a troublesome person and that they didn't want him in their lives. Still his aunt insisted that Jeremy's grandmother had driven him away and that Donald Burgess was a good man who had deserved a fairer shake from her family.

The "tough" exterior comes down as father and son embrace for the first time in decades.

When we located Donnie Burgess, a long-haul trucker who lived in Tennessee, I came down squarely on the side of the aunt. Here was a man who was not only thrilled to hear that his son was trying to find him; he'd spent years looking for Jeremy himself. Every time a delivery job took him the northern California, he took a few days off to go to Sacramento to search for his son, but Jeremy's grandmother had kept their telephone number unlisted, and he was stymied in his efforts to find Jeremy.

I was nearly as excited about this reunion as were Donnie and Jeremy. To be able to bring together a father and son after nearly forty years, when both had been actively searching for one another for nearly half that time, is more than satisfying—it makes me believe even more that I have the best job in the world.

Donnie and I flew to California, then drove to a park near Jeremy's house where I left Donnie in the car so I could first talk to Jeremy. I wanted to make sure that he would be comfortable with a surprise reunion with his Dad and quickly saw that he was ready to go forward.

Donnie not only reunites with his son Jeremy, but is surprised to learn he has grandchildren, too!

What touched me about their reunion was that while Jeremy had been the one to initiate the search, it was Donnie Burgess who strode up to his son, pushed aside the younger man's outstretched hand, which he'd offered for a formal handshake, and grabbed him in a giant bear hug. There was no question that this was a man who loved his son deeply, missed him terribly and had a lot of hugs to catch up on. So powerful was the connection between this father and his long-lost son that I found myself suddenly yearning to embrace my own father. Seeing love unfold for others always brings my love for my own family home to me.

If still waters run deep, Chad is the Atlantic Ocean. This young soldier has seen tough times, both on the battlefield and off. He deserves a miracle.

After sensing the longing people have for missed hugs from people they have loved, and watching how warm hugs can transform reunions on *The Locator*, I am now a confirmed hugger. Hugs are a wonderful way of sharing love with your family and friends. I'm still amazed at how wonderful it feels to enfold someone close to you in a warm embrace—there's a deep sense of communion, of belonging to each other that both lifts you up and grounds you.

Hugs can also be a way to reach out to people, to let them know you care about them, to help break down barriers between those unable to talk about their feelings, and to open doors to communication that might otherwise stay tightly shut. Even when people don't want a hug, it doesn't mean they don't need one. In fact, the people who resist hugs are often the ones who need them the most.

I saw this in one of our shows when an Iraq veteran decided, after his best friend died, that he had to meet the father he'd never known. His mother, who had never told Chad's biological father that she was even pregnant, had brushed off Chad's questions about his missing dad until Chad had stopped asking.

But while serving in Iraq, his best friend was suddenly killed on a routine patrol, a patrol to which Chad also had been assigned but from which, at the last minute, he had been released. Overwhelmed with grief and a deep sense of loss, Chad called his mother and told her she had to find his father for him. She was full of regrets at what she'd done to her son and contacted me to ask that we find the boy's father.

When I first met Chad at a coffee shop near his home, I

started to hug him as I always do now when I meet people, but he wanted no part of it, instead backing into a firm handshake.

To my questions about Iraq, he was distant and uncomfortable in his responses.

"We had a pretty rough time," he said, referring to his friend's death. "Are we going to get into all that?"

Clearly, this was a man who was badly in need of healing.

Fortunately, we had little trouble finding Chad's father, a fine man named Dean Cooper, who was stricken that he didn't know about his firstborn son, and was eager to make up for lost time and do whatever he could to ease the young man's pain about his friend's death and his difficult military service.

Dean embraces Chad, the son he didn't know
existed just days earlier.

We arranged a reunion for the two men, and it was a very happy day for me to see Dean, without thinking, automatically reach out to embrace Chad. But what really brought me joy was to see this young man, who had so many walls built up to protect himself from losses, not only return his father's hug but hold on tight. I saw then that he was going to be all right.

Many relationships, even ones that seem impossible to change, can be improved by hugs. When emotions run high, or when words fail, a hug can tell a loved one that all is not lost, that there is hope.

A hug says, "She doesn't hate me," " He's not unwilling to hear my side of the story," or "There's going to be a tomorrow."

It takes a leap of faith to hug, especially when you're angry, feel unfairly treated, or think you're in the right. But it can be the first step toward reconciliation.

If you've seen *The Locator*, you've seen this happen over and over again. Like me, you might not have noticed the important role hugs have in healing and bringing people together. But a simple hug can open up worlds of joy in your relationships. Try it...please.

CHAPTER 3

It's Never Too Late

One of the biggest frustrations in my work as WE tv's *The Locator* is when a man or woman turns away from the joy of a reunion by saying, "It's too late."

A man who hasn't seen his father for thirty years wonders what would be gained by meeting someone who missed out on his entire childhood. A mother worries that reuniting with a long lost daughter will only bring unnecessary pain for both of them.

But I've learned in my twenty years of helping people find loved ones that it's never too late---never, never, never. In the thousands of cases I've worked on, there has not been one case where I felt it was too late for a reunion. Even when a loved one has died, it isn't too late, because other family members can be found and healing can take place. Even when a reunion isn't the success you'd wish for, it's not too late as doors are opened to people's hearts and they can absorb the sadness of an unhappy outcome and move on in their lives.

So when a man or woman tells me it's too late, I want to ask, "Too late for what? For rebuilding a relationship, for finding answers to long-buried questions, for forgiving someone who has hurt you deeply, for sharing a new future with her?"

Some people do answer, yes, it is too late for all those things. It takes courage to face the past, especially a difficult one, and to then go forward, and there are those who, for a variety of reasons, aren't able to take those steps. But many people I meet, when guided compassionately, can embrace these life-changing opportunities and find enormous peace and happiness in reconnecting with loved ones.

I'm very sympathetic to the anxieties that can surface when I call someone to tell him that a loved one wants to reunite with him. And on television, no less! I've been a part of enough reunions to know that there are many conflicting emotions surrounding long-buried feelings—anger, guilt, deep hurt, misunderstanding, shame and fear are right up there alongside of hope, love and longing in any reunion.

But I've found that when people say, "It's too late," they're really saying, "I'm afraid," or "I'm too angry," or "Why bother?"

A parent can be daunted by the amount of time that has passed since he's seen a loved child and thinks that he can't make up for everything he's missed: the first day of school; a sweet sixteen birthday party; baseball games; school plays; graduation; a wedding day, the birth of a child.

Sometimes a child who feels she's been abandoned has managed to make a life for herself and thinks that after so many years it doesn't make any sense to revisit the past and "wreck her life."

Or, in what is a very common occurrence, a woman (or a man) feels such guilt about abandoning a loved one that she doesn't believe she deserves the joy of a reunion, even if someone is seeking her out.

So as much as my job is to physically locate loved ones, I also work hard to help the people they seek untangle their feelings so that they can understand that it truly is never too late for the peace and closure that comes with a reunion.

This was the case with Ann, a sixty-one-year-old mother who gave up custody of her daughter Shelly after a nasty divorce when the little girl was eight years old. Her daughter had been trying to find her for years, but had misspelled the name of Ann's second husband. We found this out when we took the case and were able to find Ann Koger in Jacksonville, Florida, who was Shelly's birth mother.

Ann was initially reluctant to speak to me, but finally agreed to meet me at her home. When we starting talking, she was quite matter-of-fact about relinquishing her daughter for adoption, explaining calmly that she had done it for Shelly's sake, as she couldn't care for her, while Shelly's father had a good-paying job.

Shelly relives the painful memories of her mother abandoning her at the tender age of 8 years old, after a difficult divorce.

The more she spoke, however, the clearer it became that she was haunted by the decision she'd made.

"I felt it was the best choice, but I kept wondering if it was the best choice. I have a lot of regret, a lot of regret," she told me. "I wish I could turn back the clock of time and know that I could have had some sort of substantial way of providing for her."

She kept repeating the word, "shame," in her conversation, insisting that no mother "should walk out on her kids no matter what the circumstances are." Then she began to cry as she talked about what she had missed in not knowing her daughter.

"I need her to stand in front of me and yell at me, whatever she wants to say. I need her to tell me she hated me for what I've done," she said.

Ann felt strongly that it was too late to repair her relationship with her daughter because she thought she had so badly mismanaged it, but as she talked about her feelings to me, feelings she hadn't shared with anyone, she experienced what often happens when people are willing to finally open themselves to the possibility of change—she felt a tiny, instantaneous moment of healing and hope.

*Thirty years of longing ends abruptly as Ann and Shelly come back
into each other arms and lives.*

I can actually see when this happens to my clients—the tension drains from their faces and their bodies relax as the burdens they've carried fall away. In Ann's case, facing up to her shame freed her to meet her daughter.

She was then able to understand that Shelly's motives in seeking her were just the opposite of what she had imagined. Far from telling her mother that she "hated," her, Shelly was filled with joy at reuniting with Ann. The two women embraced with all the love they'd carried for each other for more than thirty years.

This almost magical healing can even take place when the person someone is seeking has died.

Chris Szerbe of Kansas City, Missouri, contacted me for help in finding his father, whom he'd been told had abandoned him at birth. Now twenty-nine, newly married and ready to start his own family, Chris was curious to meet his Dad and ask why he had chosen not to be a part of his son's life.

I was especially eager to help Chris, as his mother's story was tragic. When she was twenty-two and Chris was a two-year-old toddler, she committed suicide, leaving him an unbearably sad note explaining that she loved her son very much but was too depressed to live. While Chris had been raised by loving cousins, I hoped to be able to help him have a relationship with at least one of his biological parents, so I took the case.

Our search went quickly but had an unhappy result. Chris's father, David Leonard, had died eleven years earlier of a sudden heart attack. Determined to help Chris find some closure, we tracked down other members of David Leonard's family, which included his two brothers, David's widow and her two children.

When I spoke to Dan Leonard, David's older brother and Chris's uncle, I had a nice surprise. Dan and his brother Mark wanted very much to meet Chris and welcome him into the family. They, in fact, thought that introducing him to David's widow and children would help heal the whole family, which was still suffering from his untimely death.

Amy explains to me why it is so important to her and her husband Chris that his father be located.

The two brothers introduced me to the rest of the

family, but I also met privately with Kathleen, David's widow, and her two children to see if they were prepared for such an emotionally-charged reunion. Kathleen told me that David had not even known he'd fathered a son, which I knew would put to rest Chris's feelings of rejection. Kristen, who is Chris's half sister, noted how much Chris looked like her Dad.

"Chris might be the last gift your father gave to you," I told her.

Knowing that the Leonard family was excited to welcome Chris, we flew them all to Kansas City to meet Chris and his new wife, Amy. While I dreaded having to tell this young man that he would never meet his father, I would be able to introduce him to the rest of the large, closely-knit family which very much wanted to include him in their lives.

Although it turned out that Chris's father had passed away,
he was able to meet the loving family of the father he has longed to know.

If ever there was proof that it's never too late, it was seeing how fully the whole Leonard clan embraced Chris and Amy, and in witnessing Chris's delight in finding uncles, a stepmother and new siblings he'd never known.

Many clients on *The Locator* have learned that it's not too late to find someone they love, to reunite with them and rejuvenate their relationships. It is rare that people, no matter how worried they were that it was too late for them, regret their decision to move forward.

Instead of carrying around the dark secret that she had harbored for so many years, Ann now has a loving relationship with her daughter, emailing regularly as they get to know each other. Chris, too, has been released from the sadness of not knowing why his father abandoned him because he now knows his father didn't abandon him--he didn't know Chris had been born. These two very dramatic shifts in the lives of these people highlight the powerful transformations that can take place when you believe it's never too late to change.

Ann, Shelly and Chris' stories can guide you to thinking about new paths you want forge. Do you want to pursue a new career, move to a new city or take a special trip? Closer to home, would you like to fix or recharge a relationship with a loved wife, son, daughter or a close friend? Do you think that too much time has passed, that it's too late to change the patterns you've adopted? Please think again.

Sometimes, of course, it is too late. I have unfortunately faced the fact that it's not only too late for me to be a middle linebacker for the Dallas Cowboys, it's too late for my fantasy that I could dream that it was possible. When it comes to our bodies, time does march on, and there's not much you can do about it.

But in our hearts and minds, in areas large and small, from life changes to personal relationships, it is never too late to grow and change. In fact, saying it is too late can become just an excuse for not having the courage to try.

No one has to tell me how hard that can be. I saw my mother struggle with the decision to look for her mother who had relinquished her for adoption, and then to face rejection when her birth mother refused to have a relationship with her. But her quest led to finding her brother, who is now a welcome part of our extended family. She rejected the idea that it was too late for closure about her adoption and is now healed and more contented than she ever hoped to be.

It is never too late to change, grow and find new joy in life. If you don't believe me, watch *The Locator*, where small miracles happen every week.

CHAPTER 4

You Can Go Back Without Looking Back

"**I** just can't go back and relive that again," a man will say to me as I work to bring him together with a relative or friend from his childhood. "That" can mean anything that he has managed to shut away in a dark corner in his mind—regret, fear, hurt or, more threatening, the memories of physical or emotional abuse, family alcohol or drug problems. He has absolutely no desire to revisit that difficult time. In fact, he wants to avoid it at all costs, even if it means refusing a reunion with a loved one.

But what he doesn't know is that you can revisit your history and control the outcome. Just as you walk carefully when hiking a narrow mountain trail so that you don't fall into a ravine, you can retrace the path to your past to recover the joy that awaits you without stepping on the emotional landmines that threaten your well-being.

When I tell people on *The Locator* that they can go back to their pasts and meet a lost loved one without looking back at the unhappy memories that may have accompanied the separation, they are skeptical, to say the least. And, before I started my career reuniting people, I, too, thought it was implausible that someone could be selective about his feelings when it came to his family history, especially if he'd gone to great lengths to bury bad and painful memories. My experience has taught me, however, that memories can be separated, good from bad, joyous from painful, and that a person is able to step way from what brings him sorrow and enjoy the powerful healing that comes with remembering loving times.

I now see that the power of love is far stronger than the need to hold onto past pain. When someone reaches out to a loved one, who we call a seeker, and that person, the target, learns that he is wanted, there is a transformation. Years of hurt and anguish can quickly disappear in a successful reunion.

Mike Grecco, Jr. was one of my clients who was very reluctant to go back when I contacted him. When he learned that his father wanted to reunite with him after a twenty-eight year separation, he wanted no part of it because he believed that his father had abandoned him as a small child and didn't love him.

Mike Grecco, Sr., had given up custody of his son during a nasty divorce that included an extramarital affair, and he was full of remorse.

When he later tried to reach out to Mike, who was only three when his father left, his sister-in-law wouldn't tell him where Mike was and directed him to send child support payments to her, which he had done. But he had not spoken to or seen his son since the boy was a toddler.

Twenty-eight years later, Mike Sr. was seriously ill with cancer and his daughter, Nicole, contacted us for help in locating her half brother on her father's behalf. He wanted to apologize to his son and make amends, she said. When I met the two of them in their home near Portland, Oregon, I saw that Mike Sr. indeed was a repentant and humble man who genuinely mourned the loss of a relationship with his son.

He explained that he had given his wife custody of Mike, Jr. because he felt he wasn't fit to take care of the boy himself, but that decision now haunted him.

"I want to right a wrong I did to him. It had nothing to do with him, and I've never stopped thinking about him," he told me.

I agreed to take the case, and set out to find Mike, Jr., who lived Concord, North Carolina. It turned out that finding him was the easy part.

When we met at a race track near his home, he made it very clear that he wanted no part of a reunion with his father. But he was open to meeting his half sister, Nicole.

Nicole weeps while telling me she wants to reunite her dad Michael with his son, Michael Jr., before he loses his battle to cancer.

Over many years of deep hurt, he had, not surprisingly, put his feelings for his father in a box and locked them away. He seemed determined not to revisit his pain, even if it meant never seeing his father again. I had serious doubts that this reunion would take place.

"As far as I was concerned, my father was dead," he told his mother after I'd broached the idea of reuniting with his Dad.

So I kept talking to him, focusing on his half sister, Nicole, and how much it would mean to her to meet her half brother. He finally agreed to fly to Oregon to see her, but would not commit to meeting his father.

"I've been thinking about it a lot, but I don't know if I'm ready," he said.

His reluctance was understandable. In his mind, his father's absence meant he had been completely rejected, so in our time together en route to Oregon I tried to steer him away from his anger and hurt and instead focus on the positive side of a reunion with his half sister and what it would mean to have a sibling who wanted to be a part of his life.

What I admired about Mike, Jr. was that when he did meet Nicole, who welcomed him with a teary embrace, he was able to put away from his lifetime of painful memories and allow her to introduce him to their father.

Just a few months after this emotional father and son reunion,
Michael Sr. passed away.

Not only that, but he listened to his father's sincere

apology, and in a very short time, forgave him. Their reunion, not at all a certainty, was heartfelt and complete. Shortly after we taped the show, Mike moved across the country to live with his ailing father. He was able to turn his back on decades of pain and anger to embrace a new, loving relationship with his father.

I've seen many clients step over truly horrible childhoods in order to find family connection and love.

This was certainly so with Vyanna Young-Davis and her brother, Addison, who reunited after an eighteen-year separation. Their childhood was one of terrible pain. Addison was removed from their home when he was three years old after suffering severe physical abuse from his father. Vyanna remained with her parents until she was thirteen, when she, too, was taken out of the home and put in foster care after her father's continued abuse. Eventually, under the loving and stable care of an adoptive family, she finished high school and graduated from college and is now in graduate school preparing for a career in social work.

At age twenty-one, Vyanna, living in San Diego, contacted us for help in finding her brother. Her older siblings had told her that she and Addison had been inseparable as children, and she remembered him as her older brother.

"I really want to reconnect with him because I've always

felt a void not having him in my life. I really feel like, if we could connect, we could be best friends again," she told me.

She was aware, even as a child, of the beatings he suffered, and was glad that he had gotten out of the house, but she had no idea where he was. The only information she had about her brother was his first name and birth date. Because of his abusive parents, any information about him was in tightly-sealed court records, which was understandable. But we were able to find that he lived in Roseville, California, surprisingly close to his sister. I contacted him.

Addison, twenty-two, was wary about revisiting his childhood with his birth family, as it had been a dark and scary place. His only early childhood memory is a recurring nightmare of his father beating him.

Vyanna downplays the extraordinary abuse which she and her little brother Addison endured before he was taken from the home at age 2. Her search for him is a celebration of survival.

"I've done a very good job of putting up walls," he said. When I asked him if he was ready to get out from behind those walls, he said he didn't know.

But, as we talked, I explained to him that if he made the decision to meet his sister, he would be able to enjoy the love and affection she had for him without revisiting the horrors of his childhood.

Vyanna and Addison are back together under much better circumstances than those they endured 18 years ago.

After talking to a friend and thinking about what I had said, he agreed to meet Vyanna and we drove to San Diego together.

Their reunion was a very happy occasion for both of these young people. They didn't ignore their sad past—Vyanna asked him gently what he remembered and they talked briefly about their parents—but they spent far more time savoring their connection.

"It's going to make the holidays a lot better, I think, just knowing that I have you around," Vyanna told her older brother. When she heard that he was planning to move from his home in Roseville, she suggested he think about San Diego.

"It's beautiful. You've got the ocean, and the people, and me!" she said.

"Those are all the reasons I need," Addison said.

That this brother and sister had the courage to defy their painful childhoods to reunite is a powerful example of how to celebrate loving relationships without reliving the pain that may have surrounded them.

I don't want to suggest that going back without looking back is simple. When a client makes the decision to reunite with someone from his or her past, he will inevitably run up against many of the feelings that contributed to the breach, such as regret, anger, fear and often deep misunderstandings. Any time there's a separation, there's a reason for it, and it's easy to get pulled back into disturbing memories and turn against a reunion.

But it doesn't have to be that way. Time and again, I've seen my clients choose not to revisit the dark events of their pasts in exchange for the promise of a loving connection. Vyanna, for instance, had plenty of good reasons to put her childhood behind her, but she really wanted to see her older brother again, so she disciplined herself not to dwell on the bad things that had happened to her and Addison, but instead, to remember her affection for her big brother and what their future could look like together.

She made a mental inventory of what she would miss if she didn't reach out to him—having a sibling at holidays, birthdays and other celebrations, sharing their lives as they grew into adulthood, being able to rely on a family member for comfort and pleasure. And now, thanks to her courage, she is enjoying her brother's company and support in the way she had hoped.

Like all the insights I'm sharing with you in this book, I've discovered that the ability to go back with out looking back can be applied apply to all areas of life, not just reunions.

In our memory banks, along with happy thoughts of shared moments with loved ones, are sad and even painful recollections: family rifts; words spoken in anger; acts of disloyalty or selfishness or harsh rejections. All these, no matter how seemingly small or subtle, can create barriers to loving relationships. As years go by, we learn to pretend these hurts don't bother us and we step around them. It can become very comfortable adapting to the compromised relationships, even though they make us sad.

Every once in a while, when you think you'd like to fix things, thoughts of reliving long-buried arguments and pushing against the patterns you've created are too daunting to even contemplate.

But it is possible to reach back to the love you have for someone without rehashing all the fights and reliving the anger that drove you apart. I've seen my clients do this many times. They acknowledge their past pain, but make conscious decisions not to dwell on it. Instead, they concentrate on full and rich futures with their loved ones.

You can do this yourself by first thinking of how you would like a relationship to be--intimate, supportive, caring, fun. Think of past happy memories of a trip, a date or an event when you and your spouse, friend or child shared joy and remember how good you felt. Imagine a future vacation where you could walk along a beach together, take a bike ride, have a picnic in a park or go to a baseball game. Think how much fun it would be to laugh together.

Once you've filled yourself with positive memories and dreams for the future, work hard to push away the resentments you feel, all the anger and frustration that has kept you isolated. This requires discipline--it's very easy to dwell on all the wrongs done to you--but I've seen so many clients successfully rise above their hurt and anger that I know it's possible. Finally, in an opportune moment and without blame, begin a dialogue with your loved one, explaining that you would like to regain the intimacy you once shared.

You can't do it alone, and sometimes the person you reach out to will, for whatever reason, slam the door in your face. But the risk of trying promises rewards you'll never receive unless you do try. And the chances are good that if you initiate a reconciliation, you will be happily surprised. So often in my work, when I've been contacted by someone seeking a loved one, and go on to locate that person, it is as if he or she has been waiting for the phone to ring. That person, the target, is more than ready to forgive and be reunited with the man or woman who is seeking him. Whether they can acknowledge it or not, most people yearn for deep connection with their loved ones, and if you can facilitate this process, you will be justly rewarded.

Impressed by my clients on WE tv's *The Locator*, I've found myself repairing friendships and family connections by choosing the positive over the negative. It's not magic and it takes perseverance, but it works. It is a very satisfying feeling to reconnect with someone from whom you've been estranged and find new pleasure in your friendship. Along with my clients, I can promise you that you can go back without looking back.

CHAPTER 5

Timing Isn't Everything

I t's remarkable how much people talk about timing when we work on reunions. It makes sense, of course, as why shouldn't time be on everyone's minds when two loved ones haven't seen each other for so many years.

But people refer to timing so often that I've had to sort out what they're trying to say to me when they bring up the concept of time. What I've found is that most references to timing can be boiled down to two main camps, the "Time-is-on-My-Side" camp and the "Timing-isn't-Right" camp. And as I have guided clients through their reunions, I've realized that their experiences are relevant to all of us as we make choices about how to conduct our own lives.

People contact me for help in finding a loved one when the timing is right for them. With some clients, the decision is straightforward, like a young woman with a serious illness who knows the clock is ticking and wants to find her father and say goodbye before she dies, or a man who has a newborn son whom he loves very much and suddenly needs to find out why his own father abandoned him at birth.

But there are many other reasons behind a client's insistence on searching for a long-lost loved one at a certain time in his life. Some have come out on the other side of bad choices or experiences, have cleaned up their lives and now want closure regarding their pasts. Some can no longer ignore their yearnings to find answers about why they were separated from loved ones. Some seem to be responding to an inner voice telling them that someone from their past is in need of help.

No matter how different the reasons are for initiating a reunion, all my clients share courage and strength in stepping out of their hurt, sadness or yearning to move forward in hopes of a better future, and it's very rewarding to help them.

It is uncanny to me how often, when the timing is right for a client (whom we call "the seeker"), it is also right for the person he is looking for (whom we call "the target"). In the most successful reunions, in fact, it can seem that the person I'm looking for is expecting my phone call. Decades after a separation, that person, whom we call the target, is often very emotional and moved, but surprisingly unsurprised to be contacted. They are eager to go forward with a meeting.

One dramatic example of listening to intuition happened in our first season on the show, when a woman approached me in a restaurant to ask if I would help her daughter find a childhood girlfriend. This is unusual; we get almost all of our requests from the mail, Internet or phone calls. But this lady's story was compelling. Her daughter, Annie, and a friend had run away from home as teenagers and moved around the country for almost a year, getting involved in some very scary situations before being picked up by the police as truants in San Francisco. There they were separated and never saw each other again.

Now, twenty-seven years later, Annie, had spent the previous year obsessively searching for her old high school friend, Nicole. Annie was an alcoholic and drug abuser, but has been clean for twelve years, and is now married and the mother of two daughters. She is a painter and teacher in Sacramento, California.

When I met her at her home, Annie told me that, at age sixteen, she had run away from an abusive stepfather, and that Nicole went with her because she didn't want her friend to be alone.

"She didn't need to run away, but she did it for me," Annie said.

They had a series of risky adventures that included being groupies in a rock band, hanging out with drug abusers and being lingerie models before they were caught by the police.

To be honest, after hearing her story, I wasn't at all sure we should help her. Compared to many of the requests we get to find children who've been abused, long-separated siblings or people with deeply sad stories, I didn't know if we should put our resources into reconnecting two girlfriends who'd had a wild fling in their youths just because Annie wanted to see her friend again. Why reward bad behavior?

Annie relives the harrowing experiences of her runaway days with Kelly, when the two girls were 16 and on the road.

So I asked her why she thought I should take her case.

"Something is telling me that I have to find her. She needs me," Annie said. "I don't know how to explain it, but she's my soul sister and I think that part of my journey through sobriety and finding another way of living is to go back and help her. I feel that she's dying."

I was still skeptical when I told my wife, Jennifer, about it, but she urged me to go forward, telling me that two close girlfriends could be as intuitively linked as family members.

So armed only with Nicole's last, thirty-year-old address in San Francisco and her name, we began a difficult search that finally led us to Seattle, Washington, where we found that she lived outside of town in an apartment where the telephone, electricity and heat had been turned off. I marveled at Annie's instinct. This did not sound like a good situation.

We left a message with a neighbor with my phone number and Nicole called. When I introduced myself and told her that someone was searching for her, the first thing she said was, "Is it Annie?" She didn't seem as surprised as I thought she'd be.

Annie had been absolutely right—her old friend was in a bad way. Just two weeks earlier, her husband had skipped town with all their money, and she and her twelve-year-old daughter were in desperate circumstances.

When we talked, I asked if she would come to Sacramento with me to meet Annie, and she readily agreed.

"I could really use a friend, and she's the only person I've ever thought of as my friend," she said sadly.

Their reunion was very powerful. These two old friends were like sisters, and they fell on each other crying and hugging and rocking back and forth.

Annie told Nicole, who now goes by the name of Kelly, that she'd been dreaming of her for two years, and wanted to help her, and Kelly unburdened herself to her friend.

Kelly walks back into Annie's life and despite over 20 years of separation, their friendship picks up right where they left off.

This was a very dramatic example of timing. It was as if the stars were aligned to bring these two women together at this particular time, when Kelly really needed someone to come to her aid and her friend wanted to pay her back for her support when they were young. Perhaps because she is an artist, Annie is more attuned to her senses and intuition than most clients I work with, but her ability to trust her instincts and risk reaching out to someone from her past is an example everyone can follow.

Another case where timing was shared by both the seeker and the target was that of Andrea Tuchten, a twenty-four-year-old woman from Queen Creek, Arizona, who contacted us to find her birth mother. She'd been given up for adoption when she was three days old. While her adoptive family was loving, supportive and able to give her everything she needed, she had always felt a void in her life, as she knew that her birth mother had an older daughter whom she had kept.

When I saw the video she sent to our office, I could see the deep pain in her eyes, and decided she needed help in finding some answers.

When we met, I saw that I was right.

"I always ask myself, 'Why was I the one who got pushed away and out of the picture?' I don't know why I was the bad one," she told me.

Her insecurities had led her on a downward spiral, and she had been a drug and alcohol abuser as well as a runaway, but for the previous three years she'd been clean and sober and now very much wanted the closure she thought could come by meeting her birth mother.

I was concerned that a bad outcome to this reunion—that her mother would not want to see her, or was dead—would send her back to her dark past, but she assured me that she was strong enough to face the truth, so I agreed to take the case.

What I found when I contacted her mother was that Andrea had been right to call me when she did. Her birth mother, Mary Lazano, had been looking for Andrea as well. "I've never forgotten about her. I was trying to find her last year and I didn't have any luck so I kind of gave up on it," she said when I reached her on the telephone. I could hear from her voice that she was crying.

I suggested that the time might be right for her to meet her long-lost daughter.

"Oh, yes," she said.

When we met near her home in Laredo, Texas, she told me that she had been forced to give up Andrea for adoption, and missed her terribly. Divorced from her husband, who had custody of their daughter, she had an affair and got pregnant with a man who left her. She knew she couldn't support Andrea so, through a friend, she found a wealthy couple who wanted to adopt a child. She drove by the house where her daughter would be placed, saw that it was a gracious home in a well-to-do area of town and took some comfort in knowing her daughter would be taken well care of. A lawyer successfully arranged the adoption, and Mary felt she was doing the best thing for her baby. But she was heartbroken that she couldn't keep Andrea, whom she'd named Jennifer.

"The worst part is walking out of the hospital with your hands empty," she said.

Now remarried to her ex-husband and a mother to a teenage son in addition to her two daughters, she was more than ready to meet Andrea, so she and her older daughter flew with me to Phoenix. Before I introduced them to Andrea, I met with Andrea to make sure the young woman was ready for this major change in her life. She promised she was, so Mary came out on the patio where we were standing and wrapped her daughter in her arms.

"I held you so tight before I had to let you go, just like this," she said to Andrea. "I'd like to just take you home. We're finally together. It feels great to hold you."

Andrea's years of self-abuse ended the moment this hug began.

It was obvious that these two women were at the perfect

times of their lives for their meeting. Andrea was mature enough to understand the reasoning behind her mother's decision to put her up for adoption and young enough to enjoy years of a loving relationship with her. Mary, too, was settled in her life and able to devote herself to building a relationship with the daughter she'd never known.

This was good timing at its best.

Lunch with Andrea, who expresses her hope for a successful search.

Ironically, as important as good timing can be in arranging reunions, it is also one of the most common reasons people give for rejecting a reunion.

When I call a target, I can tell pretty quickly if my call is bringing welcome or unwelcome news because one of the first things I hear from someone uneasy about a reunion is the timing.

"This isn't a good time for me," or "I'd rather wait until my mother is no longer living," someone will say to me, which means he is afraid of letting my client into his life again.

It's not my style to insist that a target meet a long-lost relative or friend--a person has every right to turn me down-- but I've learned that talking someone through the excuse of bad timing and onto the more substantive reasons why he cannot go forward with a reunion clarifies the situation for him. Sometimes a person will then decide to reunite and sometimes he refuses, but at least he knows why and isn't using time as an excuse.

The "Time-is-on-my-Side" camp and the "Time-isn't-Right" camp categories aren't just helpful for sorting out reunions on *The Locator*; they are worth analyzing when making decisions about our own lives.

Blaming timing for not doing something, for instance, is almost always a bad idea.

Too often, when we procrastinate in the face of doing something we don't want to or are afraid to do, we simply say it's not the right time, as if that explains everything.

A man is uncomfortable saying the words, "I love you," to his wife or children and therefore rationalizes that it's never quite the right time to speak up. You want to lose weight, but it's the holiday season and you're going to too many parties, and you put off your diet. You'd like to learn to fly a plane, or scuba dive or take a gardening course at the local high school, but it's too hard to make a definite commitment every week, or you think you shouldn't waste the money, so you never make the phone call.

Instead of letting opportunities slip away, I suggest you ask yourself what I ask people on my show. When is the right time?

If now isn't the right time to tell your wife you love her, when is the right time? If you're throwing away a flyer outlining a cooking class that sounds like fun, when is the time to take the course? If now isn't the right time to sit down and work through a serious disagreement with your son, when is the right time?

Turning this excuse on its head will help you see that you can go forward with things you need or want to do without waiting for some magic time. There is no magic time—there's today, tomorrow, the next day and the day after that, each there for you to live fully. The sooner you take action, the better.

Similarly, just like people on WE tv's *The Locator,* we can pay attention to our own clocks. In watching people on the show respond to their instincts when they look for a loved one at certain times in their lives, I've realized that the same intuition is available to most of us who pay attention.

I'm one of those people who believes that everything in life happens for a reason. Hearing from an old friend who wants to meet, finding a want ad for a job that you'd like to apply for, watching something on television that leads you to plan a trip to a new vacation spot can all be signs that move you in a new direction. If you are comfortable trusting your own good sense and intuition, you will be able to take advantage of the good timing that is offered to us all. You will be open to new things, better relationships and a richer life in much the same way as my clients.

CHAPTER 6

There Are Three Sides To Every Story

One thing that constantly surprises me when I am trying to facilitate a reunion is how often people have the facts wrong. Little bits of truth get passed around and rearranged to create an overall history that simply isn't the way it was. Over time, someone has heard the story told so often and with such conviction that it has become the reality for him or her.

A daughter is convinced that her Dad is a deadbeat, a son blames his mother for driving away his father, a daughter thinks her mother loves a sister, more than her because the mother kept the sister but gave her up for adoption. These misguided beliefs, so closely held, can make anyone, no matter what age, feel unloved, deeply hurt and angry.

When I hear both sides of a story, one from the person who's asked me for help in seeking a lost relative or friend and the other, sometimes completely opposite story, from the person I've found, one of my biggest challenges is to guide both the seeker and the target away from the inaccuracies in their individual stories to the third story, which is usually closest to the truth. If I can persuade each person to let go of the falsehoods he's been led to believe are facts, and then to shed the accompanying anger and anguish that have haunted him, we can usually go forward to a rewarding reunion.

Sorting through the stories to find the truth can be heartbreaking. It is painful for someone to realize that he has based most of his beliefs on the wrong story. But, with this knowledge comes a tremendous sense of liberation when he embraces the truth.

This happened in a reunion between a mother and son, Warren Stone and his mother, Carol. Her daughter, Holly, contacted us to help her mother find the son from whom she'd been separated for twenty-eight years.

Carol's story was a sad one. Her former husband had physically abused her, and when, after repeated beatings, she kicked him out, he took their two-year-old son, Warren, with him. Because it was his father who took him, the social services agencies Carol contacted at the time wouldn't go after him, and she was too frightened of her ex-husband to look for Warren on her own.

"I had great fear from him and his family," she told me when we met near her home in Rome, New York.

She had remarried and had two daughters, but was haunted by the son who'd been taken from her.

"My mother never forgot about him for one day. He's always crossed her mind. If he comes back into my mother's life, it will fill a hole. She needs that closure," Holly told me.

Carol still seemed to be suffering from the loss of her son. She was very anxious and found it difficult to leave her house. When I visited her there, I smelled alcohol, and asked her if she had a drinking problem.

"I'm not going to deny it," she told me, adding that three or four beers eased her days and relaxed her.

So we made a deal that I would try to find her son if she would try to stop drinking, and I set out to hold up my end of the bargain.

Finding Warren wasn't difficult. In fact, he lived twenty minutes away from me in Cape Coral, Florida, so I called with the news that his mother was searching for him, and he agreed to meet me.

I was surprised that one of the first things he told me when I asked him what he thought about his mother was that he hoped she wouldn't be disappointed in him.

"If she were to be disappointed in who or what I've become, then she can just find what she's done for the past twenty-eight years… no contact," he said.

When I suggested that he sounded angry, he agreed.

"A lot of anger, a lot of animosity," he said. "Maybe it was too much responsibility, maybe she felt it was going to be too hard for her. I'm really not sure, but all I know is that I really could have used her help throughout my life.

"My true feeling is that she abandoned me. She gave up on me. I have three boys of my own and I couldn't imagine not seeing them again, especially not for twenty-eight years."

Taking a walk with Warren to discuss the possible ups and downs of his pending reunion with his biological mother, Carol.

I reminded Warren that the reason I was in his living room was that his mother had contacted me to find him, and that he had been taken from her against her will. He was able to hear me, the first step in letting himself understand that he might not have the whole story.

At the end of our conversation, after I told him how much his mother wanted to reunite, and how sorry she was for the time that had passed, he was ready to meet her.

"I'm really looking forward to sitting down with her and trying to get to know her, hopefully to have some kind of relationship with her when it's all done," he said.

He also asked his father, who lived with him and his family, if he regretted what he'd done, and his father said, "No."

"That's heartbreaking," Warren told his father. "Well, either way I'm going to go meet her. I'm going to talk to her."

He agreed to fly with me to upstate New York, where Carol and Holly were to meet me in a local park. They had no idea he was with me when I walked over to say hello.

The first thing I asked was whether Carol had stopped drinking, and she had.

"You don't know how hard it was…but I did it," she told me. "It meant an awful lot to me because you said that if you're going to try, then I'm going to try. That inspired me an awful lot and made me feel good."

It meant a lot to me as well that she had trusted me and what I was trying to do to help her and her son. When I realized the discipline it had taken for her to stop drinking, I had a good feeling about the reunion. Both she and her son had already moved away from their old beliefs and had taken important steps towards each other.

A few minutes later, they were in each other arms after nearly three decades.

They had a lot of catching up to do. Warren's childhood with his father had not been easy, which had been Carol's fear, and she apologized for not being able to help him.

"It's not your fault," Warren told her.

This is the moment I made a deal with Carol that, if she will fight to get clean and sober, I will do my best to locate her son Warren.

Warren was able to let go of his anger and resentment when he understood that he only knew part of the story about his parents. And when Carol could apologize to her son for all the years she'd missed, she could forgive herself.

"Now that we have you, you aren't going anywhere—not out of my life," she told him. "I'm looking forward to every step, every conversation."

Warren and his mother now speak every day and have plans to visit with their families. They are creating the third side of their story together.

I'm not implying that finding the third side of the story is always easy. It requires strength and forgiveness of the highest order to give up the beliefs you've carried for years, and even heartfelt reunions can't always quickly heal what time has put in place. This was so with Angel, a woman whose ex-husband had given away their twin sons without her permission.

Angel was forty when she contacted us for help in finding her sons, but she had only been fifteen when she started dating a man more than twenty-five years her senior. She was sixteen when, pregnant with twins, she married him.

"The judge who married us said to her former husband, 'If she wasn't pregnant and her mother wasn't sitting beside her in the courtroom, I'd have you arrested,'" she told me when we met in Tucson, Arizona, where she lives with her second husband, Dan.

She and her first husband separated when her twin boys were fourteen months old because her husband was violent.

"I did it for the boys; I didn't want them to grow up thinking that's how men treated women," Angel said.

Because she had no means of support—not even a high school diploma—she moved in with her father to get her life back together and her husband took custody of the children. She had regular visitations with the boys, named Taylor and Tylor, who lived in Washington state, and relocated there for six weeks every summer from Oregon to be with them. Soon after one of these visits, her former husband's daughter called to warn her that he was trying to give up the boys for adoption.

"'Tell him good luck with that, because I'll never give away my rights.' I told her," she said.

But when she went to Washington to see her sons soon afterwards, their father had moved away with the children, and had left no forwarding address. Since that time, she had had no contact with the twins, who were now the same age she'd been when she'd last seen them.

"I think of them every day, sometimes just in passing, sometimes just an ache," she said. "I feel like they were stolen."

She paused for a moment, and added, "I've never stopped loving them, and I don't know how to move on from here. I just want a little piece of them."

Because she had their Social Security numbers, I was able to find the boys fairly quickly. They were living with adoptive parents in Puyallup, Washington, and when I contacted their mother, Ruth, she was not happy with my call.

I met her and husband, Jim, at their home, and she was very wary of my visit.

"We lived in a little world that was safe. I felt like we

lived in a little bubble, and then there was a crack," she told me of my call.

This is the beautiful but tormented face of Angel, who is desperately seeking her twin boys, Taylor and Tylor, who were taken from her.

She explained that she and her husband couldn't have children of their own, and a friend had called from her church saying a man wanted to give his twin sons up for adoption. When the boys spent the day with them, she and her husband knew they wanted to raise them.

"Their father told us that their mother had left when they were two years old," Jim said. He added that the man had promised to send them baby pictures of the boys and more information, but they had never heard from him again.

"The boys are so wonderful and amazing to me. They are a gift," Ruth said.

She and her family were always anxious that someone

would come to the door looking for the boys, maybe their father or mother or a private investigator.

"On Mother's Day, I always wondered if their mother was hurting, and we had a moment of silence for her," Ruth said.

The boys themselves also thought their mother had abandoned them. They wanted to meet Angel but were nervous and also worried about Ruth.

"I'm loyal to her and don't want her to feel that we don't love her because we do," Taylor said, but they very much wanted to go to Tucson to see their birth mother.

Ruth came along as well. She said she wanted to support her sons, but I wondered if she needed to be there for her own sake.

When we got to Tucson, I met with Angel and her husband first, without the boys. I told her that I'd found her sons, and showed her their high school graduation pictures.

She cried and clung to her husband while she admired the picture of her handsome young sons.

And when they walked up behind her, she was overwhelmed, hugging them for a long, long time and then sitting them down, peppering them with questions. It was wonderful to see her wide smile as she drank them in, and they responded with tears and smiles as well.

When Ruth appeared, Angel thanked her for taking such good care of her sons, and Ruth told her that they had thought of her every Mother's Day.

As they filled in the gaps of their separate narratives and the third side of the story emerged, however, the women had a hard time. Taylor and Tylor, when they learned that their mother hadn't abandoned them and had, in fact, yearned for them every day, were moved and excited to include her in their lives. For them, the third side of the story brought closure to their questions about their parents. But it wasn't as simple for Angel and Ruth.

Angel was clearly shaken when she heard how easily her ex-husband had given her sons away.

"I never gave my permission for an adoption, and I was always looking for them," she told Ruth. "I gave birth to my sons to raise them."

Ruth, who had embraced the boys thinking their mother had abandoned them, was shocked to learn that Angel believed her sons had been stolen from her. Ruth had thought she and her husband were doing the right thing for the boys, so it was hard to hear that the truth was not as comforting.

After the reunion, Angel planned to visit the boys in Washington, and sent Ruth a small present, but the two women have not been in contact. The real story, which is that both women are dealing with the effects of an illegal adoption, will take some time for both to absorb. Embracing the third side of the story, as this case vividly illustrates, often calls for a great deal of forgiveness and healing.

Because I spend so much of my time sorting through the often completely contradictory stories surrounding the reunions

I arrange, I have seen how easy it is to get the facts wrong. There is usually a grain of truth that starts a chain of assumptions that leads to a misconception and then a wrong conclusion, and it can take a long time to help people unravel all this to discover what really happened.

But what I've realized over the last twenty years is that it's not just people who haven't seen each other in many years who buy into these false stories. We all have a tendency to see things through the too-narrow lens of our own feelings, needs and biases, believing only our side of the story, sometimes at the expense of the truth.

While this can be very familiar and comforting, you're selling yourself short in the long run. Considering other versions of every story is a way to more fully take advantage of a situation and expand your thinking and horizons in the process. The reality is that there are just so many reasons why people say and do things that it's crucial not to take any important interaction at face value.

What if you've just been turned down for a job you really wanted and think you said something wrong in the interview, or that your resume wasn't strong enough or that the interviewer didn't like you? You're discouraged and reluctant to send out your resume again because, what's the point?

But what if the human resources person had a completely different agenda that had nothing to do with you? What if he'd been told not to hire someone as well qualified as you are because the company wants to keep down salary costs, or that the company gives preference to in-house hiring or that he really wanted to hire you but he just found out that the son of a company board member wants the same job?

There are always three sides to every story: yours, the other person's and the one in between. It's very much in your best interests to walk yourself through all the possibilities of an encounter. The result will be a much clearer picture of what's going on, which will in turn lead you to the best way to handle a situation.

When you have a problem at work, a fight with your spouse, a disagreement with a friend, stop and think. What could be another version of this story? Did my wife mean to hurt my feelings when she snapped at me or is she just anxious because her mother is visiting? Does my boss really expect me to stay late to finish a project or does he simply not know how long it's going to take? The more questions you ask yourself, the better choices you'll make.

I've helped thousands of people change their lives by guiding them to look at the three sides of their stories to find what's really true. It is very empowering to be able to step outside of your viewpoint and explore every other way of looking at a situation. When people can do this, regardless of the outcome in a particular incidence, they are helping themselves grow and learn and make more informed decisions about everything— their relationships, their careers and their dreams. Please, like our clients, try it.

73

CHAPTER 7

Stubborn People Lose Out

A lot of people ask me if there are ever sad endings on the WE tv's *The Locator*, when the person we're looking for simply says no, I don't want to meet my daughter, my son, my father.

The answer is yes. There are some people who have locked down their feelings so securely, either because they are very angry or very ashamed of their behavior toward someone in their lives, that a potential reunion seems a terrible threat rather than an opportunity for happiness.

Fortunately, these truly stubborn people are few and far between. But the havoc they create in the lives of others, and the healing that they deny themselves make them stand out in my work. The days I run up against them are not good ones for my clients or for me.

The first stubborn person I encountered was close to home. My first search in what became my career as *The Locator*, in fact, was to find my mother's birth mother. Katie Dunn, who is now the chief investigator for our company, asked me to find her mother, who had given her up for adoption as a baby. And I did find her, but when I did, the woman refused to have anything to do with my mother or our family.

The rejection was devastating for my mother. Ultimately, she came out on the other side of her sadness, was able to move on with her life and was glad she'd found closure. In her case, happily, her half brother learned of their mother's behavior, contacted her himself and now she and the rest of our family have a wonderful relationship with him. But coming up against that wall of rejection was not easy.

An amazing echo of that first rejection came in one of our shows when Scott Bass, a mechanical engineer from Tomball, Texas, contacted us to find his half brother after he learned that his mother had refused to acknowledge her firstborn in her life.

I went to Tomball to meet Scott, who told me that his mother had told him she'd received a call from a son she'd put up for adoption.

"She said that he was forty-one years old and had called her for medical information. She also said that she would rather I didn't talk to him if given the chance. Really, the only reason she told me was because she was afraid that I would find out from him, you know, that he would call me," he told me.

Scott went to see his mother and learned that she'd had a baby when she was nineteen. She deeply regretted what had happened, had put the baby boy up for adoption and reiterated that she would rather Scott have no contact with him.

This didn't sit well with her son, however.

"I would like to know more about him. I'd like to meet him. His is my brother, you know, and the rejection he got wasn't from all of us."

So, without his mother's knowledge, he'd contacted us.

He acknowledged the risk he was taking by going behind his mother's back.

"I'm concerned that it could mess up my relationship with my mother," he said. "I'm risking a lot. I just hope it's worth it."

When we found Donald Dozier, who also lives in Texas and who now goes by his middle name of Keith, it was clear that his mother's rejection had hurt him deeply. When he called her to ask for some medical information, she wouldn't even get on the phone to speak to him. It was her husband who gave him the information he needed.

"I could say it hurt a little bit," he said when I pressed

him for his feelings. "But then I've been going through it for forty-one years so I try not to think about it too much."

Scott tells me how the rest of his family rejected contact from his long-lost brother Donald but says that he was not going to slow down his search for his missing brother.

Then I asked him how he felt about the fact that his half brother was seeking him out after hearing about the rejection he suffered from his mother.

"My wife keeps saying, 'You have a brother. He's your blood,' but it doesn't really compute," he told me.

Yet, later, in talking to his wife, after he'd had time to think, Keith was able to appreciate the generosity of this unknown man.

"When you've got someone who totally shuts you down, rejects you and then someone from that same family turns around saying, 'You know what? If you're not big enough to do that then I'll step up and do it.' And he did."

I went with Keith, his wife and two children to meet Scott and his family, and found it very moving to see these two men together, one in pain from his mother's rejection and the other eager to soften that pain.

Scott was very happy to find he had an older brother and Keith thanked him for taking the risk to find him.

"I want you to know that you may not feel welcome in all the family, but at least in my part of the family you are welcome," Scott told his newly-found sibling.

Brothers at last. Scott and Donald embrace for the start of a life long brotherhood that remains solid to this day.

In both of these cases, family members stepped in to ease the blows of a harsh rejection and, in doing so, have expanded and enriched their family circles.

More difficult is when no one can cushion the anguish of complete rejection, which happened to a young woman named Wendy from Tucson, Arizona, who contacted us to find her mother.

Wendy's mother had abandoned her and her brother to their paternal grandmother and aunt when they were ten and nine years-old, respectively.

Because she had spent the first decade of her life with her mother, Wendy had lots of memories that made her yearn to see Wendy's mother again.

"I just want to know if she thinks about me on my birthday. I think about her on my birthday," she told me tearfully, when we met near her home.

Wendy's mother was white and her father was black, and they went through a bitter divorce when Wendy and her brother were small. After a hard-fought custody battle, her mother got Wendy and Christopher and, soon after, her father committed suicide. Then her mother remarried a white man, and, slowly, Wendy and her brother began to feel marginalized by her mother, stepfather and the new children in the family.

"We started to become the outsiders instead of the insiders. I hate to say it, but the way it seemed to me was that it became that we were black kids being raised in a white family," she told me.

"I remember my stepfather's family coming one time and me and my brother having to go to our room because of some reason, but we pretty much stayed there all day."

When she was ten, she and her brother were put on a plane to visit her paternal grandmother and aunt in Tucson for what her mother told her was a short visit, and that was the last time Wendy saw her.

Wendy remained with her father's relatives, and is very fond of them, but had a difficult adolescence and early adulthood that included alcohol and substance abuse, marriage and divorce. Now, however, she is free of her addictions and wanted to see her mother again as an adult.

Sadly, this was not to be.

Initially, I couldn't find Wendy's mother, but I did find her father-in-law. He refused to help me, but inadvertently gave me the clue I needed to call Wendy's mother at her office.

I couldn't get past her assistant, however, so left my number and asked that Wendy's mother call me on a very personal matter. She did telephone me early the next morning, and we did not have a good conversation. She seemed horrified that I had located her and didn't ask me one question about her children.

I was left with nothing for Wendy, until a few days later when Wendy's mother wrote me a letter to read to her daughter. She explained in the letter that because she had such bad feelings about her ex-husband, she couldn't see Wendy or Christopher and wished them a good life. She did not say that she loved her children nor did she sign the letter.

This was going to be tough. Now matter how old and mature someone is, being turned down by your own mother is painful beyond measure. One of the most important parts of my job as *The Locator*, at least as important as arranging successful reunions, is doing all I can to ease the pain of a bad rejection and help someone move forward.

I met with Wendy and told her that her mother was not coming to meet her, but had written a letter to her and her brother, which I read.

She was stunned when I was finished, forced to face the fact that her mother was not interested in seeing her. I was worried about her because she seemed to measure her feelings of self worth by her mother's disappearance, and this letter was not going to help.

My experience has taught me that even when there is a poor outcome of a reunion, the seeker eventually profits from knowing the truth and is gradually able to make peace with her past. My mother was able to do this and so have many others with whom I've worked, and I told this to Wendy.

"It's really important that you take this and move forward with the rest of your life. You cannot wait for this woman to come around. She can no longer be empowered with the ability to tell you your worth," I said.

"It's so unfair," was all she said.

Telling Wendy that her mother, who I located, did not want to see her. Hands down, the most heart breaking moment of my 21-year locating career.

Her mother's rejection was a big blow and I spent a good deal of time with her, talking her through her sadness. Slowly she seemed to be able to listen to me.

"I can't leave here without knowing that you're going to be okay," I said.

"I'm going to be okay," she said finally. "Trust that. It may not have turned out the way we wanted it to but it is a milestone that really will matter."

The carnage resulting from a rejection is hard to repair, but most people who've reached out to loved ones and been turned down are eventually glad they found answers. This was certainly the case with my mother and with other clients, who were able to stop yearning for something that was never going to be and instead concentrate on the many people in their lives who did love and cherish them.

In fact, it is my belief that the biggest losers in an aborted reunion are the stubborn people who turn away from reconnecting with loved ones from their pasts. It's not that they are unjustified in their feelings. Many times someone who refuses a reunion has every right to be angry about how they've been treated. An absent father who forgot every birthday, never acknowledged important milestones, like sports achievements, high school or college graduations, or a wedding leaves a lot of anger in his wake. Why should his daughter welcome him with open arms?

Or, what is more common than one would think, people turn away from reconnecting with someone because they are so ashamed of their own behavior. Birth mothers who've given up their babies for adoption have sometimes completely suppressed any memories of an unwanted pregnancy and are appalled when contacted by the child they gave away. Because they hate themselves for what they did, they assume that their son or daughter will hate them as well.

Everyone has the right to refuse a reunion, of course, but the high-intensity encounters I have with these truly stubborn people—fury at my call, a threat of legal action, or simply hanging up on me—reflect a lot of unresolved feelings that can eat away at them. Holding on to legitimate anger against a parent or other loved one from the past can feel right, but if that person is searching for you in a true spirit of forgiveness and love, what's the point in being "right?"

Similarly, the guilt that keeps others from accepting a reunion offer isn't going to disappear by itself. A man knows he made bad decisions and is so ashamed that he doesn't want any connection to the person he wronged. But what he doesn't know is that it's extremely rare for someone to go to the trouble of contacting me solely to seek revenge. It's quite the opposite. Someone initiates a search to get answers, to find closure and renew a loving relationship.

I listen carefully to the people who say they don't want to reconnect with the person who wants to see them because not everyone who says, "no," really means it.

In fact, so many people who initially aren't interested in a reunion change their minds that we've named the phenomenon for record-keeping purposes—it's called a "soft rejection."

These are the people who, when I reach them on the telephone, are very quiet and say only a few words because their brains are spinning with the news I bring. This is completely understandable. After all, the people seeking them have had plenty of time to think; the targets have had none, so it takes awhile for them to sort through the history of their relationships, remember the causes for the separation, and decide whether they can forgive, apologize and then embrace a long-lost loved one.

As we talk, they slowly begin to realize the possibilities that will open up for them if they do reach out to the person seeking them, and most of the time they are ready and grateful for the chance of a reunion.

But there is a small group of people who have built up

such high walls around themselves that I don't even get the opportunity to talk to them. They are the ones who get very angry when I introduce myself and have no interest in what I have to say.

Hearing these stubborn people cling to their negative feelings, shutting away important parts of their lives, has made me eager to help others from going down the same path.

Many of us find it strangely comforting to nurse old wounds and feelings of guilt rather than to face up to them and let them go. It seems impossible to forgive someone who has treated us badly, or to find the courage to apologize for something we've done, so we do nothing. Time passes and we become more and more locked up in the excuses that can justify our behavior. We become the stubborn people I see on *The Locator.*

Why? Why do we resist, when taking a deep breath and reaching out from behind our walls can bring such amazing rewards of love and communion?

Fear, disappointments in life that have beaten us down, self-preservation from past rebuffs or failures are all legitimate reasons that keep us from trying. But I can promise you from the cases I've worked on that if you can truly say, "I'm sorry," or "I forgive you," or "Let's try a new way of thinking," nothing but good things will happen to you.

If you are skeptical about changing old, stubborn habits, go slowly. The next time you're about to criticize your child, compliment him instead. When you get home from work and are about to plop down in front of the television with a bag of chips, lamenting the extra pounds you're packing, take a walk around the neighborhood.

These small steps might seem insignificant, but once you have gotten comfortable with small behavioral shifts, others will follow. You will find you have the confidence to make bigger changes—speaking up to a boss who treats you unfairly, repairing a relationship with an estranged friend. You will begin to see the world in a different way, slowly expanding your horizons, and reaching out to others with a more open and trusting heart.

The difference between my clients who are open to rethinking their pasts and embracing new beginnings and those who slam the door on any change is startling. Stubborn people define themselves by the injustices they feel have been heaped upon them or by the guilt they have about their own behavior. Their world becomes narrower and smaller as they age. Those who can reject these limitations are so much happier and full of life. You can watch them on WE tv's *The Locator* and choose for yourself who you'd like to emulate. You know what side I'm on.

CHAPTER 8

Blood Is Not Always Thicker than Water

How often we hear that nothing is stronger or more dependable than the bonds of family. I certainly find it true that my relatives (most of the them, anyway!) are my most steadfast supporters, whenever I need them. Without my wife, children, mother, brothers, sister and other uncles, aunts and cousins, my world would be a very empty one.

But I've learned as the WE tv's *The Locator* that love and commitment to one another are not exclusive to those sharing the same DNA. When I first began my work, I was surprised by the number of requests we received from people seeking to find someone from their past who was not a family member.

A veteran wanted to reconnect with someone from his unit, a woman yearned to reunite with a childhood friend who had supported her during a bad period with her own family, another woman felt closer to her godmother than to her stepmother.

What set these requests apart from those of clients seeking family members was that they pleaded their cases more aggressively, as if they had to go the extra mile to persuade me that their claim was legitimate.

"He is more than a brother to me," they would write, or, "No one in my family would have done what she did for me."

As we read these letters or watched videos, I began to understand that the urgency of the requests reflected a bias our society has against intimate relationships outside of familial ties. It is assumed that "blood is always thicker than water," so these people, in asking for our help, had to press their cases with extra intensity.

They were right to do so, because, at first, without knowing it, I was one of the people who bought the myth that DNA took precedence over everything. I'd never considered that friends could be as close as blood relatives.

A case that helped my blinders come off was when a young woman named Samantha Johnson asked us to find her godmother, Hattie Gallaway.

Samantha, who grew up in North Carolina, lost her mother as a small child, and her father remarried a woman with a child of her own. Her father was in the military and often deployed for long periods of time, her stepmother was busy with her own child and a new baby in the family, and Samantha was drawn to Hattie, a neighbor and young mother who had more time for Samantha than did her own family.

When Samantha contacted us, she was thirty-three and living in Sacramento, California. A single mother of three children, she had come out on the other side of an abusive marriage, had gotten a college degree while working full time, was now somewhat settled, and very much wanted to reconnect with Hattie.

I wasn't sure about taking the case because Hattie was not her birth mother, but my team persuaded me that, to Samantha, Hattie was her mother.

When I met her at a park near her home and heard the way she talked about her godmother, I agreed.

"Hattie was there when my stepmom could not be there for me. She took me in and made me a part of her family, and was there for most of the major events that happened, such as school plays and school recitals. On summer vacations we'd go up to her Mom's house and stay there for a whole month, and everyone treated me as if I were her daughter," Samantha told me. "She taught me the things I needed to know."

Samantha vividly remembered the last time she'd seen her godmother, which was when Samantha was moving to

California with her father, stepmother and half siblings.

"She made me a picnic lunch and gave me some roses and the biggest hug I could ever remember. She asked me if I really had to go," Samantha recalled. "She said, 'You can stay with us.'"

I asked her why she wanted to find Hattie at this point in her life, and Samantha said she very much regretted losing touch with her godmother—"I just stopped making that one phone call and then her number was changed--," and wanted to have her in her life again.

Samantha had clearly bonded with Hattie as a daughter to a mother, and I agreed to try to find Hattie for her.

This wasn't the easiest search we'd ever had as Hattie had divorced and remarried, so I went to Madison, North Carolina, which was her last address, and actually found her by walking around the small town and showing her picture to everyone I met.

"That's Bunny," said a man I met at a stoplight, and I knew it was the right person as Bunny was the nickname that Samantha had used for Hattie.

When I pulled into Hattie's driveway, I saw that I was at the home of a very loving person, because there were family members everywhere, sitting on the porch, on the steps to the house, on the lawn outside.

Hattie told me that Samantha was a girl of ten when they first met at the playground near both of their homes. Hattie was there with her young son, Devin, and Samantha came over to play.

"I think Sam adopted me first, and then we adopted her," she said, explaining that Samantha's new baby brother garnered most of the attention at her house, and that Samantha was having a hard time.

"She started to call me, 'Mom,'" Hattie said. "I'm so thankful that I was there to be able to talk to her when she came with questions. She became the daughter I never had."

Hattie happily agreed to meet Samantha, and their reunion was a joyous one for both women. Their obvious devotion to each another was a big lesson to me, showing me that love and commitment are not exclusive to family relationships.

Hattie and Samantha, the god mother and god daughter that taught me blood is not always thicker than water.

Another non-family reunion taught me that the strong bonds of friendship can even extend beyond life.

Warren Withrow sent us a video asking for help in locating the daughter of his best friend, a woman who had died of AIDS two decades earlier.

He had met his friend Tracy when they were both in their twenties and had instantly become friends.

"The first time we met we started sharing stories and I just connected with her right then. She was infectious with life. Her passion, her laughter were wonderful," he said, when we met near his home in Charlotte, North Carolina. Their relationship was platonic—she called him her "little bro" and he called her his angel— and they became like family to each other.

At the time, Tracy had cleaned herself up after a very dark period in her life when she had been addicted to cocaine and had been a prostitute. Sadly, during that time she'd become infected with the HIV virus, which became AIDS. When she and Warren met, she knew she was living on borrowed time. She also had a baby daughter named Sara, to whom she was devoted, and Warren shared in the baby's care.

"I loved Sara as my own," Warren told me, describing how happy he and Tracy were when Sara, who had been born with the AIDS virus in her blood, suddenly stopped testing positive for the virus and was clean of the virus, a highly unusual occurrence.

As Tracy neared death, Warren wanted to adopt Sara, but was not in a position to care for her, so he and Tracy searched and found a good home for her.

"Tracy made me promise that I would stay in Sara's life," Warren said, and after the baby was placed with her new family and settled in, he planned to do just that. But when he felt it was appropriate to reconnect with her, he couldn't find her. The family had moved away, and he'd been searching for her ever since.

"I want to find her so I can fulfill my promise to Tracy, who was a wonderful person. She wanted Sara to know how much she loved her. I have that message, that information."

I was very moved by Warren's story. He was clearly devoted to his friend's memory and wanted to do right by her daughter. He was acting very much like a loving brother, and I wanted to help him honor his pledge to Tracy.

Warren ponders the promise he made to a dying friend and then failed to keep.

Sara had been adopted in Santa Barbara, but her family had moved to Fort Worth, Texas. Her adoptive father had then left his wife, and she had been raised by her adoptive mother, Diane, in a single-parent household. When my mother, our lead investigator, contacted her, Sara asked that I speak first to her mother before talking to her.

Diane described a troubled young woman who had wrestled with her family history.

"Death was a part of her life, because of her mother, and she's never really been able to bond. I know she loves me, but she's never gotten too close," she said. Diane hoped that when Sara met Warren she would be able to put to rest the demons surrounding her mother and reconnect with those who loved her.

"She feels that she's missing something. She needs to feel complete."

Sara said nearly the same thing to me when I met her soon afterwards.

"I'll get close to somebody and then they're gone. I've had a lot of people walk out on me—my adopted father was one of those people. I thought that if they left then I'd done something wrong. That's why I push a lot of people away."

But she was willing to meet Warren, whom she didn't remember, because of his connection to her mother. What she'd heard about Tracy was mostly bad, that she'd been a drug addict and a prostitute, so when I asked her what she would like to ask Warren, I wasn't surprised when she said, "The good things about her. Did I make her happy?"

I was very glad to be able to help grant her wish.

I took Sara with me to Charlotte to meet Warren. Before the reunion, I explained to Warren in private that Sara had had a tough time, and he was very regretful that he hadn't been in her life earlier. He promised me that he would make sure she stayed connected to him so that she could learn about the good side of her mother.

Making good on his promise to his dying friend, Tracy, Warren reunites with Sara and vows to watch over her the rest of his life.

Theirs was a very successful reunion. Warren warmly embraced Sara as he told her how much her mother had meant to him, and how much Tracy had loved Sara. He produced baby pictures of Sara that she'd never seen, and started the process of helping Sara know her mother. Sara was curious and grateful to have her early life explained to her.

Cases like Warren's powerfully illustrate how people can connect outside of traditional families. It's not just blood ties that draw people to each other, but a shared view of life, a natural affinity for one another that grows to a close and a mutually supportive relationship.

The key to all successful and intimate relationships is that people invest in those they love. They put in the time to listen to each other, help each other and enjoy each other. This is why adopted children who want to find their birth parents are at the same time loyal to their adoptive families, the ones who got them vaccinated, drove them to soccer games, made them to do their homework and were always there to support them. Likewise, both Samantha and Warren felt loyal to the people who had invested in them and made them feel whole.

I admit that I had to be taught to appreciate the power of non-familial relationships. Now, like any convert, I'm eager to spread the word to others to urge them to honor and embrace their connections with friends outside of their family circle.

I've seen enough reunions between old friends, army buddies and high school sweethearts to understand that caring and intimate relationships are not bound by blood. The joy and love that come when these people reconnect is no less heartfelt than the feelings in reunions between family members.

We are the sum total of all the people who have passed through our lives, including our parents, grandparents, spouses and children, but also our friends. In fact, because we can choose our friends, they can feel closer to us than some of our family members, offering sympathy, companionship and emotional sustenance that we sometimes don't get from our relatives. They talk, laugh and listen in an open and objective way, allowing us to even complain about our families!

I admire the people who contact us for reunions with non-family members because they are bucking the common assumption that friends aren't as important as family. They recognize the value of their friendships and they want to restore and rekindle them.

Maybe you have some friends that you've neglected, let slip away, or simply take for granted. Spend a little time thinking about them, how they've supported you, and what you mean to each other. Hopefully, you don't need *The Locator* to find them and let them know how much they mean to you.

CHAPTER 9

People Actually Can Change

W hen I tell people that some of the greatest reunions on WE tv's *The Locator* have never happened, people assume we can't find a person being sought.

That's not true. The most common reason for a failed reunion is that the person we find refuses to meet the person who's seeking him. Time and time again, a target will insist that the person who wants to reunite with him cannot have changed.

This response is very frustrating. Our culture celebrates transformation and change. Book stores bulge with self-help books, and a click on the Internet yields classes, gurus and programs that promise to guide people to self-improvement.

And people do believe in change—in themselves. Many people can see themselves changing, but aren't willing to recognize or honor change in someone else. I will meet a target who mentions that he's stopped smoking or recently changed careers, but when I bring up the person who's seeking him, that same person will refuse to believe that another can change as well.

"A leopard can't change his spots," he'll say, or "You can't teach an old dog new tricks."

Not only is this attitude hypocritical; it is heartbreaking. Anyone who has made even simple changes in his life—cutting down on caffeine, parking the car far from a store to get more exercise—knows that shifting behavior requires daily commitment and discipline. It isn't easy. And many of the people I meet haven't made just small changes. They had serious alcohol or drug problems, suffered from depression or anxiety and have worked very hard over many years to put their demons to rest. They want nothing more than to apologize to a loved one for past behavior and to have a chance to improve their relationship.

I work like crazy to get the person a client is seeking to open up his heart, explaining that a father, brother, sister or son is a completely different person. I try to persuade him or her to give a loved one the chance to say he is sorry. Far too often, however, a target is unwilling to let go of years of anger and hurt, so a reunion, if it takes place at all, can be very rocky.

One such case happened when we were contacted by a man who wanted to find his daughter, Rebekah, whom he hadn't seen for fifteen years, since she was three years old. Robert had been a terrible father, addicted to drugs and alcohol, and abusive to his wife. She divorced him, which did not stop his bad behavior.

"I was drinking a lot and doing drugs and not caring, " he explained to me, when we met at his home in Dickson, Tennessee. "I was really getting hard into the drugs and when Trish came over one time to pick up the child, during one of my visits with her, she saw me strung out and took Rebekah away. That was the last time I saw her."

Robert said that he continued his drug and alcohol abuse for several more years.

"I was living in a pit and, about seven years ago, I climbed out of it," he said.

Now clean and sober, he wanted desperately to apologize to Rebekah.

"Maybe she's old enough and adult enough to hear my side and hear me apologize to her for not being there for her whole life," he said. "If I just get forgiveness, that will be enough."

Robert's mother, Joyce, echoed her son's description of himself.

"He was a nasty drunk," she confirmed, and added that Rebekah's mother had moved in with her when Rebekah was small and that she, Joyce, had helped take care of the family during that difficult time.

But, she went on, her son had worked hard to clean himself up and she thought he deserved a chance to reconnect with his daughter.

I very much believe in second chances and felt sorry for Robert, who had dug such a deep hole for himself, so I took the case.

Rebekah, when we found her, was a freshman at the University of Arizona, and not at all pleased to hear that her father was looking for her.

Rebekah had been told so many negative things by her mother, it was difficult to convince her to consider meeting her father.

Her opinion of him, based exclusively on what her mother had told her, was that he was a really bad guy.

"Growing up, I didn't know my Dad. He was abusive to my Mom, he was a drug addict. He was not a good person from what I know," she said, adding that he'd never sent her a birthday card or called on Christmas.

I explained to her that all that she had said could be absolutely true, but tried to open her mind to her father's side of the story, which was his journey to sobriety, his deep regret that he had neglected her, and his desire to make amends.

"I'm not a forgiving person," Rebekah told me firmly. Because of her father's behavior, she said, she had difficulty trusting other people, afraid that they, like him, would leave her in the end.

I suggested that if she was able to repair the relationship with her Dad, then maybe she would feel freer to pursue other trusting relationships, something I've seen happen very often after a successful reunion, but she seemed skeptical.

To my surprise, however, she did agree to fly with me to Tennessee to meet her Dad. I decided to bring her grandmother Joyce to the reunion as well as I hoped that her presence might ease the meeting between Robert and his daughter.

When we got to Dickson, I first reunited Rebekah with Joyce and the two women embraced warmly. Joyce was very eager to get to know the granddaughter she hadn't seen in so many years. She asked after her mother, and Rebekah told her that her mother wasn't speaking to her because she'd decided to come to Tennessee.

"Gosh, your mother and I were such good friends," Joyce said sadly.

While they were talking I went outside to see Robert who was waiting there. I told him that Rebekah was a very angry girl.

"This is not going to be one of those magic-moment fixes when everything gets better. You broke her heart, slowly but surely over fifteen years, and it might take you fifteen years to fix that heart," I warned him.

He said he understood, and was ready to go forward.

Their reunion was very painful. Rebekah wouldn't make eye contact with him until he started to apologize to her.

"I wanted to tell you I'm sorry," he said, but she interrupted him in a flash of anger.

"Sorry's not going to cut it," she said, and told him she hated him.

"I'll gladly let my grandma into my life, but not you," she told him, and he stood up from where he was kneeling and left her and her grandmother.

Joyce asked Rebekah to give her father a chance to make up to her, and Rebekah didn't answer.

"If you didn't care you wouldn't have made this trip," Joyce said.

I agreed and applauded this young woman for her courage. Agreeing to a meeting, no matter how unsatisfying it turns out to be, is one small step towards reconciliation. Many other older and supposedly more mature people than nineteen-year old Rebekah refuse outright to even consider meeting a loved one.

Those people won't meet with me, or even talk with me over the phone. They are sticking to their side of the story, and there is no room for change.

Then I have to return to an extraordinary person who has done everything to turn his life around, and tell him the bad news that the person he's seeking doesn't believe he's changed and refuses to see him. These are the shows you don't see on television.

Some of the people who turn down reunions are just too young. They hold on to righteous anger because they still see the world in simple black and white terms. From their point of view, they were wronged and there is no reason to change their position.

They also aren't familiar with forgiveness. They usually haven't done anything terrible for which they needed to be forgiven, so find it hard to forgive others. Young people also sometimes turn down reunions because they haven't experienced enough loss in life to realize the importance of their family connections. They're not old enough to understand the value of maintaining a long-standing good relationship.

Others have any number of reasons for refusing a reunion. Some have been so scarred by their history with a loved one that they sincerely cannot believe that person is capable of acting unselfishly. Others have allowed themselves to become defined by their anger and don't really want to give it up. A woman whose husband left her for her best friend sees no reason to hear her ex-husband's side of the story because it might involve taking some responsibility for the breakdown of her marriage. Others are very judgmental about someone who wronged them—they prefer to hold that person's feet to the fire rather than give them the benefit of the doubt, let alone forgive them. Whatever the reason, the answer is no, no, no.

But these people unfortunately don't see what I see, which is how powerfully the human spirit can be when driven by the need for another's love. Anyone who saw Robert put his hands to his face and cry when I told him that Rebekah had agreed to meet him could see how hard this man was working to try to earn his daughter's love after so many years of neglect.

In Robert's case, there is hope. Rebekah, furious and hurt as she was, defied her mother and showed up to hear her father's side of the story. She allowed a little crack of light to shine in on their relationship, which is the beginning of healing. Now, in fact, she is texting her father daily and they are planning a trip together.

Where there is the will, change is always possible, and my work has taught me to honor the many people I see who make big changes in their lives. Some, like Robert, have taken radical steps to rid themselves of addictions and reach out to find loved ones in hopes of reconnecting with them. Others are those I call to explain that someone from their past is seeking a reunion. In those conversations and meetings, they choose to let go of their guilt or anger or fear and agree to reconnect. This, too, represents a big shift in their lives. They are giving up strongly-held beliefs about someone in order to consider another viewpoint.

Really, all the work I do on *The Locator* is about change. A person contacts us because he wants to change his life for the better by finding a loved one he cherishes, and the person who gets my phone call and agrees to meet is open to change as well.

I then can see how two people can open up to a new ways of sharing and communicating. Love, healing, intimacy, a new, shared future, expanding family relationships all accrue from successful reunions.

If you are someone who is skeptical that people can change, look in the mirror. Whether learning to use new technology like computers, cell phones and GPS systems, adjusting to a new boss at work, moving across country, watching your child march off to her first day of school, facing the sudden death of a friend, you are changing all the time. You are a different person than you were five years ago, or indeed, than you were yesterday, because you are responding to and adapting to the world around you.

And so is everyone else. Your spouse loses her job and goes back to school so she can change careers, your son suddenly decides he doesn't want to play football anymore and takes up soccer, your daughter breaks up with her long-time boyfriend, your friend leaves a bad marriage.

Change is inherent in life. It's part of the human

condition. It makes little sense to believe that people don't change because nobody doesn't change.

And if someone is particularly motivated, he or she can make very big changes in life. You've probably made a few yourself, so why can't others do the same?

I've learned that, "You can't teach an old dog new tricks," simply isn't true. I've seen long estranged parents and children renew their love for each other, siblings reconnect, people close to death determined to right the wrongs they've visited on loved ones.

Embrace change, both in yourself and as importantly, in others.

CHAPTER 10

Broken Hearts
Know No Boundaries

As those of you who watch WE tv's *The Locator* know, our clients reflect the wide diversity of our world. Rich, poor, young or old, people from all walks of life contact us because they all share the same need to connect with missing family or friends, have questions answered and resume loving relationships.

But there is one niche of people set apart from all my other clients—those who are very famous; the people you see on television, in the movies, on the front pages of the business section or in the halls of Congress.

People sometimes are surprised when I tell them that we

have quite a number of famous clients, as if celebrities somehow don't suffer the same losses and pains as do the rest of us. That's not true. Oddly, my celebrity clients, the ones with huge homes, or even several homes, swimming pools, and private jets, whose names are splashed all over the news, are sometimes the people who need these reunions more than many of my other clients. For them, reuniting with long-lost loved ones provides a connection to their old, true selves, something they don't always have in their glittering world.

Great success and celebrity bring with them many good things—fulfilling work, money, a glamorous lifestyle, privileges not available to the rest of us, and access to an elite club of fellow achievers. But I've learned that the less desirable aspects of fame--the constant glare of publicity, the need to always put on a positive, public face and the danger of false friends who are more interested in the trappings of a person's success than in the person himself—can make it hard for a celebrity to reach out to find someone from the past who is important to him.

When they do reconnect with someone from their past whom they've been yearning to see for many years, it can be especially sweet, a real gift in what are sometimes remarkably isolated lives.

There is a big firewall between famous people and the rest of us. Hangers-on, paparazzi, people wanting access to the world of celebrity can be relentless and unscrupulous in trying to befriend famous people, so celebrities usually surround themselves with employees whose primary job is to protect them from the outside world. Compared to most of us, who move freely from home to office to supermarket to the park or to the mall, greeting people as we go, celebrities can have surprisingly little contact with anyone outside of a small circle of trusted employees, family and friends.

As "The Locator," this means that a famous person rarely calls me himself. Unlike my other clients, who send letters, videos or emails and communicate with us directly, I will get a call from someone in the star's entourage, and that person will tell me his boss wants to hire me to find a loved one, but that I cannot talk to the famous person in doing so.

I don't work this way. I can't. For a successful reunion, I need to hear, in the seeker's own words, his story and why he wants to make this reunion happen. It is the only way I find out what issues we're dealing with, take the emotional temperature of a given situation and know whether I'm going to be able to bring him together with the person he seeks.

If we get past that hurdle, we discuss privacy. In our business we always honor a person's wish for privacy, but in the world of celebrity, the importance of secrecy becomes paramount. A slip could mean that an intimate meeting between a famous film star and her birth mother could be fodder for the tabloids, with embarrassing ramifications for all. I understand and completely agree with a celebrity's insistence on remaining discreet. We always offer to sign a non-disclosure agreement and never, in twenty years of locating, has my office revealed the identity of someone who has wanted his reunion kept secret.

If all this meets with the satisfaction of person I'm talking to, he takes his information back to his boss. Most of the time, the celebrity soon calls me, eager to move forward with a reunion.

This is when I can begin to do my job, because the minute I speak to him on the phone, his fame, for me, disappears, and he immediately becomes like all my clients—a person who has carried longing, sometimes deep hurt and many unanswered questions in his heart for many years. Also, by the time he has summoned the courage to call me, he is usually very open to my questions and in touch with his own feelings.

Even in the beginning of our connection, though, I'm sensitive to certain issues unique to this privileged class.

First of all, celebrities are very busy, which means that arranging phone calls and meetings can be complicated. Further, when we do talk, we usually have to cover a lot of territory in a short amount of time.

The fact that they lead such full lives also means that celebrities, more than my other clients, have often been able to totally suppress their feelings about a long-lost loved one by submerging themselves in the demands of their careers. Making movies, running for office, going on international tours combined with all the glamour and attention that surrounds their work can swallow huge chunks of time and be very good excuses for not thinking about the pain of a lost connection, and, more significantly, persuading them that these connections aren't really that important—"Why should I worry about someone from so long ago when I've got everything I want?"

As a result, many years can go by before they confront the missing pieces of their lives. All of my clients, to some extent, spend too much time pretending to themselves that deep pain and a sense of loss about missing loved ones will eventually disappear, but celebrities seem to corner the market on deep, deep denial, so that when they finally do open up and face their past, it can be very, well, dramatic. They are celebrities after all.

Secondly, famous people have to show a carefully crafted public face to the world, one that excludes any self-doubt, unhappiness or uncertainty. They can never not seem to be in control, and the constant pressure to look and act happy when they are sad and lonely can make them feel like they're living a lie.

"I have to cut you off now," a prominent politician told me during an emotional phone conversation about a potential reunion, "I have to go to a press conference and pretend to be happy."

Often, I'm one of the few people to whom a celebrity can unburden himself about how much he longs to see someone from his past, and my heart always goes out to these very famous clients who have to wrestle so privately with their anguish while acting as if they're on top of the world.

Further, when we find the person being sought, we have to tread carefully because of the fame factor. In the initial contact on a celebrity's behalf, I never reveal his or her name to the target. Only with permission from my client do I later divulge his identity. Some people react with complete shock and then enthusiasm to the news that a famous person wants to reunite with them. Some, usually older people, take the information in stride by being happy but not particularly impressed by our client's stature. Some seem like they knew the news all along.

This happened when actress Melissa Gilbert asked us to find her biological family. I located them for her, and before telling them very much, asked if they had any idea what their daughter might look like now.

"I've always thought she would look like that actress on Little House on the Prairie, the middle sister," said one relative. "That actress looks like our family."

Melissa was incredulous when I told her and couldn't wait to meet her birth family.

But sadly, in other cases, there are targets who are scared off by a person's celebrity. Ashamed or feeling unworthy, they refuse to meet the famous person who wants to reunite. I then have the unhappy task of reporting back to our client that his success has worked against him.

But when the reunions are successful, famous people react with the same joy and sense of closure and peace that all our clients do. I take great pleasure in seeing people in the public eye after we've arranged a reunion for them and knowing that their sunny public persona is matched by a new, inner peace.

The large majority of our famous clients insist on privacy, and I understand why. There is little to gain and much to lose for a celebrity who goes public with the news of a reunion, especially in sensitive cases. I've helped a famous actress reunite with a child she gave up for adoption and who wants to protect her daughter from prurient publicity about her mother's long-ago affair. A well-known musical star hired us to who find her estranged brother, but wants to keep their new, warm relationship private as she realizes that he would not be able to handle the glare of her mega watt fame. Another client is a major action movie star who reunited with his birth mother, a woman who wants no part of the publicity that surrounds her son. When we conduct searches for these people, in fact, we don't use their names—even my staff knows such a case only by a number. Privacy is paramount.

There are some famous clients, however, who share their stories of reuniting with loved ones and friends with the public.

Film start Ray Liotta, who was adopted when he was six months old, announced publicly that he wanted to find his birth mother, hoping that someone seeing him would help him locate her. When that didn't yield any results, he contacted us, and we were able to find his birth mother, who had given him up for adoption at the age of sixteen as an unwed mother. When they reunited, he learned that she had put him up for adoption, not because she didn't want him, but because she loved him enough to allow him to be adopted into a stable family who would be able to give him a better life. This was exactly what he needed to hear after a lifetime of worrying that he'd been an unwanted child.

Actress Melissa Gilbert has also talked publicly about

her need to find her biological family after the death of Michael Landon, the actor who played the role of her father in the long-running television show *Little House on the Prairie*. He had been her surrogate father off-screen as well as on their show, supporting her after the death of her adopted father when she was a young girl. When he died of pancreatic cancer at age fifty-four, she was devastated at the second loss of a paternal figure. It was then that she made the decision to try to find her birth parents and called us for help.

When we met and talked, I very much wanted to help her as, after the double loss of important men in her life, she really needed answers to the questions about her birth family. Happily, when we found them for her, they were very supportive and delighted to have Melissa in their lives.

After we helped singer Rozonda Thomas, better known by her stage name Chilli as a member of the R&B girl group TLC, find her father, she allowed the Sally Jessie Raphael to share their meeting, a very emotional journey.

And recently, when I was appearing on the television show The View with Barbara Walters, she shared with her audience the successful search I conducted for her a number of years ago.

I admire these famous people who risk unwanted scrutiny of their personal lives by talking publicly about their search and reunion experiences. It is hard enough to face the uncertainties of a reunion when it is a private affair between family members or estranged or missing friends. Reunions are always very powerfully charged events, bringing together people with separate histories, varying perceptions about each other and not much more than hope that things will turn out well. You're never quite sure what's going to happen.

So, for these celebrities to allow the public into their private, emotional journey, knowing that many eyes will be watching and judging them takes a tremendous amount of courage. And, besides being courageous, I think they are very generous, in using their fame and the public platform it provides to talk about their own successful reunions, they show the way to others who may be longing to initiate a reunion but are hesitant to take the risks of not finding the person they're seeking or of being rejected if they do find someone.

When people learn that stars like Melissa Gilbert, Chilli and Ray Liotta have found answers to a lifetime of questions and now seem to be at peace, it can inspire them to start their own searches for loved ones.

I have seen so many lives become fuller and richer with the love that comes from successful reunions that I always come down on the side of sharing the good news that reunions bring. So when a celebrity is willing to say so, too, I say thank you and keep up the good work. You cannot have too much love and happiness in the world.

CHAPTER 11

You Can't Find PEACE Until You Find All the PIECES

The reason that I use this phrase to open my show every week is that this is where my work begins and ends. Many good things happen in successful reunions. There is the tremendous happiness of reconnecting with a loved one, relief to be able to share your feelings after so many years and excitement about what the future will bring.

But underpinning the intense emotions that surround any reunion is the deep and abiding sense of peace that comes with finding answers to questions people have had for most of their lives. Getting the pieces of your past back is the purest and most satisfying outcome of any reunion.

If your life has unfolded without painful separations from your loved ones, it is hard to understand what a huge hole there can be in your heart from not knowing your past. You know who your parents are, where your siblings live, keep in touch with friends from high school and college. You have confidence that comes from knowing where you came from as well as the assurance that you can find out anything you need to know about the past and what made you the way you are by simply asking your family.

But imagine, instead, that in the back of your mind you're always wondering if a missing father ever thinks of you, whether the daughter you put up for adoption is in a happy home, or if your sister, from whom you were separated when you both went into foster care, is alright or even alive. These are the kinds of questions that people have if they've lost contact with loved ones, and years can go by without ever finding the answers. They live with a distracting and ever-present anxiety, just enough so they can never quite be at peace, and never quite be in complete control of their lives.

To be able to help people reunite with those they yearn to see again and have their life-long questions finally answered is one of the greatest rewards of my job. I watch my clients let go of the burdens they've carried for years and almost instantly relax into a fuller sense of who they are, no matter what the outcome of their reunions.

Paul Spicer, thirty-three, was a NFL football player with the New Orleans Saints when he contacted us looking for the father he'd never known. He had a very successful career, a loving wife and four children, but was very much a person who needed to find the pieces of his life.

"I want to find my Dad," he told us when he sent us a video to ask us to help him find his father. "When you're going through your life and you don't know half of who you are—I need to know."

NFL star, Paul Spicer, sits with his wife in their living room and contemplates the shocking news I have just delivered to him.

I drove to Jacksonville, Florida, to meet Paul and his

wife, and he explained that his father left his mother before he was born. He was very articulate in expressing his deep longing for a family connection.

"Four years of high school when I was all-American this and all-state that and there was nobody in the stands—no family," he said.

Now the father of four children of his own, he wants to be a good father, but doesn't know how.

"I know I can be better. I know that I can. But when you're basically teaching yourself, you're going to make a lot of mistakes and I've made 'em," he said.

I wanted very much to help Paul, but we found out that his father had died in an automobile accident, so our team then searched for any other family members we could find to help Paul learn about his father and his own roots.

When I met Paul's Uncle Edgar and Aunt Nanette, who lived in Austin, Texas, I learned that it was likely that Paul's father didn't even know he had another son.

"I was blown away to know there's someone out there who's a part of our family and we didn't know about it," Nanette told me.

"He was driven," she said of her older brother, "and sometimes the drive got in the way of him being the father he could have or should have been."

Edgar wanted to help his nephew.

"He does have a right to know who his father was and does have a right to know he has brothers, sisters, aunts and uncles who do care," he said, when he and his sister agreed to fly to Jacksonville to meet Paul and his wife. They also told me that Paul had a half sister named Kristina, who, like Paul, had not known her father, so I invited her to join us in Jacksonville as well. Since I couldn't bring Paul's father to him, I wanted to introduce him to as much of his family as I could.

I met Paul again without telling him that his unknown family was with me because I wanted to first tell him his father had died. I knew it was going to be a blow to him to discover he would never have the chance to talk to the man he'd spent his life yearning to know. All I had was a photograph of Charles, Sr.

"It's hard," he said sadly, looking the picture, "and the hardest part is deciding what to feel for somebody you never met, but whom you wanted to meet and you don't even get the opportunity to."

Then he asked me if I had any information about any other family members, like brothers or sisters, and I was very glad I was able to tell him that yes, I did, and that they were standing outside in his driveway.

When Nanette practically disappeared into the arms of this big NFL defensive end, she laughed.

"This takes me back to when I was little and looked up at my big brother," she said. "Wow!"

Paul thanked his newfound relatives for coming to see him.

"Whatever it was in you to say, 'yes,' and to come, I can't ever express in words how to thank you for even coming here because you didn't have to."

"If you've ever been thinking or wishing or just hoping and dreaming of something for your whole life," he said, "people talk about dreams not coming true and that stuff doesn't come true—my wish today just came true."

Paul is now in regular contact with his aunt and uncle and has found his missing siblings. While he will always carry a lingering regret that he never met his father, he is learning more about him through his newfound relatives and has truly has found peace by finding the pieces of his life.

It's wonderful when people have their questions answered and can use that newfound information to guide them to the next stage of their lives. When people reconnect happily, they and the person they've found can rebuild their relationship, making up for lost time and creating new memories together.

This happened when Cindy Ruff contacted us to find the son she'd put up for adoption when she was nineteen. An adoptee herself, she had gotten pregnant by a high school boyfriend who did not want to share in raising the baby. Unable to care for the baby by herself, she reluctantly gave her son to a family through an adoption agency run by her church. Now forty-one and married with three children of her own, she was anxious to know that her firstborn had grown up loved and taken care of in a happy home.

"I hope I made the right decision because I would be just devastated if I found out otherwise. I don't think I could live with the guilt if he was abused or if they didn't love him growing up, that would be horrible," she told me when we met at her home in Bakersfield, California.

Cindy need not have worried. Her son, Daniel, when we found him in Utah, had grown up in a very loving home and described himself as "super happy," with wonderful siblings and a great mom. He, too, had questions for his birth mother--if he had any siblings, what his dad was like, why she put him up for adoption.

I take a moment to tell Cindy that I believe the courageous decision she and other birthmothers make is heroic in my eyes.

He was eager to meet his birth mother and came with me to California, where he met Cindy, her husband and their three children, his half-siblings. It was a happy reunion. Mother and son, who looked remarkably alike, bonded immediately and Daniel and his new siblings also took to each other--Daniel and one of his new brothers discovered they both played the drums. Daniel's adoptive mother joined them, too, thanking Cindy for letting her have Daniel.

Cindy and Daniel's questions have all been put to rest now, and they will be a part of each other's lives in the future. Cindy is in touch with Daniel's adoptive mother and is flying to Utah for a baby shower for Daniel's new wife—"you're going to be a grandmother!" Daniel told her. They have both found the missing pieces of their lives.

Cindy finally knows she made the right decision as soon as she wraps her arms around her son, Daniel.

Even when the outcome is not what I'd wish for a client, however, and there is no reunion, there is comfort and a sense of empowerment in knowing the truth.

One of the most difficult cases I worked on, that I talked about in Chapter Seven, was when Wendy, from Tucson, Arizona, learned that her birth mother refused to reunite with her. She was devastated by the news, as she had spent a good part of her adult life seeking to reconnect with the mother she'd known for the first ten years of her life.

But finding out how difficult a person her mother was, though painful, was also liberating for Wendy. She began to understand that the reason she and her mother were apart was not because of her own failings, but rather because of the kind of person her mother was. She then better understood her grandparents' reticence about her mother--she'd blamed them for trying to hide something from her, but realized that they had really been protecting her from her mother. She began to appreciate that, in living with her grandparents and aunt, she had grown up with better people than her mother.

In that single swoop of a moment when her mother's rejection hit her, Wendy began to heal, and start to take control of her own life.

There is usually a trigger that motivates someone to start looking for the missing pieces of their lives; a father with a serious illness wants to make amends with a loved one before he dies; a daughter who has cleaned herself up after years of drug abuse wants to find her birth mother as part of her effort to move on with her life; a sister laments the fact that no blood relatives were at her college graduation and wants to find the brother who was put in foster care; a daughter who has heard only bad things about her missing father from her mother wants to find out what he's like for herself.

But, behind whatever timely reason motivates a call to me is a lifetime of questions about the unknown parts of a person's life. The questions range from big ones to small ones. An adopted woman doesn't look like anyone in her family and wonders if she looks instead like her birth mother. A son can't understand how could his mother possibly have left him in the sole care his father, as she must have known he was physically abusive. A woman who, as a child, was taken suddenly from her foster home thinks she did something terribly wrong to cause her foster mother to turn her out so abruptly. A daughter whose father dropped her off after a weekend visit when she was thirteen with a promise to take her on a vacation, but never returned—why? A son wants to know if his birth mother likes music as much as he does. Another adopted son wonders what his life would have been like if his mother had kept him.

The touching aspect of all these questions is that they are being asked by adults, but they are really the questions that children ask as they grow up.

Think of the millions of questions you asked your parents when you were small, and the answers you received, everything from where did your awful freckles come from, to why are you so uncoordinated in sports, to why did your grandfather die at such a young age. Imagine what it must be like for someone who has those same questions and has had to carry them around in his head for his whole lifetime without anyone to answer them.

Finding the pieces for these people is far more complex than simply satisfying their curiosity. It is the only way for them to finally feel in control of their lives, to have a full sense of who they are and to move forward with their lives.

We can all take a page from my clients who are not afraid to look for answers. They go forward with reunions hoping that their questions will be met with the responses they want, but there are no guarantees. That they want to pursue the truth even if it means discarding a lifetime of beliefs is very brave.

Most of them, however, would be the first to say that the payoff is worth it. Everyone deserves to know all the pieces of their lives and find peace.

Final Notes

One of the great pleasures of being WE tv's *The Locator* is meeting people who are fans of the show. In the grocery store, on a plane, in a restaurant, at a gas station or at the mall, people often approach me to tell me how much they like what we do. Some have seen the show once or twice, but many people who come up to say hello watch it regularly and know almost as much as I do about the clients we've helped. It is clear when they talk about their favorite, successful reunions or express their regrets at the reunions that ended unhappily that they have embraced the sense of forgiveness, hope and joy that is at the heart of our work. Their understanding and support means everything to me, and I am very glad when they take the time to let me know.

Along with their affection for *The Locator* is a continuing curiosity about how the show works and what it's like to be *The Locator*, and I thought it would be a good idea to end this book by answering some of the most frequent questions people ask when we meet. I'm happy to spread the word about how we've crafted this successful program and the wonderful people who make it happen every week.

1. Do you read, listen or watch every request for a reunion?
Yes. Every single letter, video or tape that we receive gets the full attention of our staff.

2. How do you pick a case?
There is no single way that we choose a case, which is one of the reasons I think we are able to help such a wide variety of people. I am drawn to cases where a person could really use a miracle in his life, someone who's been to hell and back and needs some good news: a woman who, while giving birth to a daughter she had to give up for adoption, contracted a virus that made further pregnancies impossible, and wants to locate her one child; a young woman whose abusive childhood was like something out of a horror movie and really wants to find the older brother who tried to keep her safe.

Also compelling are requests from those who have worked very hard to change their lives, like someone who's kicked a bad drug or alcohol habit, and wants to apologize to those he hurt or abandoned along the way.

Any case that has a "ticking clock" aspect, like a terminal illness, or a major life change like a marriage or birth that's about to take place, catches my attention. A timely reunion can have a tremendous impact on the lives of family members, bringing them together at a very important time.

Cases we don't take are those from abusers, either physical or emotional, or from deadbeat dads who left their families and never sent any financial support.

One question that people often ask is whether we choose a case based on whether or not we think it will be easy to solve, and the answer is a resounding, never! The reason we don't isn't just that it wouldn't be right, but that over the years I've found out that there is no way to predict which cases will be solved and which ones will not. I've seen seemingly impossible cases, where all we've had to go on is a misspelled last name, solved very easily while other cases loaded with information and leads end up with a permanent question mark. My job, I've learned, is to use my experience and intuition to choose the cases I think most worthy and then go forward with an open heart and mind.

3. Is it hard to keep your own feelings in check during an emotional reunion?

Yes, sometimes it is very hard. I meet people when they are very vulnerable, often scared and hurt, and, when a reunion isn't going the way they've hoped, it is very difficult to not to share their anguish. But, if I lose my emotional grip it does a disservice to the people I'm trying to help. Throughout our work together, they need to see that I believe that the reunion is going to work, or they will lose confidence themselves.

At one point, when I was having a bad time with this, I asked a surgeon who operated on very sick children how he managed to go to work every day without getting overwhelmed by the sadness of some of his cases.

"I can't deny the humanity of someone's pain, but I can postpone the dealing with it," he told me, explaining that he tried to maintain professional equilibrium in front of his patients and their parents and then retreated to the privacy of his office to let his feelings out.

I attempt to do the same, always focusing on the goal at hand, which is to guide people to forgiveness, healing and connection with a loved one without letting my own feelings get in the way.

Most of the time I'm successful, but when my own emotions do threaten to spill out into a reunion that hits close to home, I sometimes keep my sunglasses on to protect my myself from unraveling in front of a client.

4. Why do you walk away so quickly after a reunion?

The reason I leave is because the reunion isn't about me. It's about the people who have given so much of themselves to each other and have worked so hard to forgive each other and start a new relationship together. I am a facilitator and my role ends when they meet. They don't need me anymore, so there's no need for me to hang around. I would just be in the way.

5. What happens when you do go?

I head home as quickly as possible. I leave the set immediately after a reunion—I don't see what happens afterwards, in fact, until the show airs. My crew has a car ready—a different car than the one I came in so no one will know it's me—and like the crew at a car race, they've got the engine running, the GPS programmed back to the airport and a tuna fish sandwich and a cold drink waiting for me. I call my mother, our senior investigator, to tell her what happened and then I call my wife to begin the transition back from *The Locator* to being a husband and father, back to the atmosphere of the Dunn family.

Every heartfelt reunion makes me so grateful for my own loving family that I can't wait to get back to them.

6. What about the crew? How do they feel about the show?

This is very interesting. We have a relatively small crew, no more than ten, compared to other shows that can have upwards of thirty or more people. We have to keep the crew small because of the intimate nature of the show—we are going into people's homes and filming mothers, fathers, sisters, brothers, aunts, uncles and close friends at their most intimate moments. The last thing we need would be an army of technicians clanking around, banging into lamps and messing up carpets while someone is sharing their deepest secrets.

Further, I know I'm biased, but our crew is one of the best out there. We've kept the same people since our first episode, four years ago, which is unusual in television. Many of them could be making more money on another, bigger network show, but they want to be a part of the good news we see on *The Locator*. They are very sensitive to the intimate nature of the reunions and do their jobs unobtrusively and skillfully. I'm lucky to have them.

7. How is it working with your mother?

Terrific. I could not have a better senior investigator, mother or not. I started my business because of her so, in a way, it's like the completion of the circle to have her with me now.

She brings to our searches an amazing tenacity that I think is partly a result of the fact that her own reunion with her birth mother never happened. In a way she is always looking for good things to happen for others that she couldn't have happen for herself.

I feel some of that too, wishing when I report back to her the happy news of a successful reunion that I could've done the same for her.

8. How does your family feel about being a part of the show?

My family, especially my wife Jennifer, is the most under-appreciated part of *The Locator* experience. I don't know that when she signed on to marry me that she had any idea that she was going to be the wife of *The Locator*. We have a big family, seven kids, and she works at maximum capacity when I'm away from home. I feel a fairly significant amount of guilt about that.

But she's involved in all our cases—we talk about them together and she's eager to know how they turn out. And my oldest son,

Trey, is interested in continuing what is now the family business. He wants to expand it internationally.

9. Are you surprised that the show is so successful?

When I really think about it, no. I think seeing a happy reunion awakens something deep inside each of us, a yearning to forgive our differences, to open our hearts to another, to love and be loved. Watching how joyfully people embrace each other after years of separation—talking, laughing, crying with such happiness—allows the rest of us to believe in redemption and communion. It also inspires people to look into their own relationships and improve them so they can enjoy the same new intimacies and deep connections they see on *The Locator*. At least I hope that's what happens!

10. What happens to people after the show is over? Do you follow up with them?

At this point, we have no formal follow-up procedures with those who have appeared on *The Locator*. Sometimes a client will go on another television show or talk show to share his or her experiences, but, otherwise, we feel that since they've so generously given of themselves to our television audience that we should respect their privacy and let them be. But it is an interesting idea. I'd like to know that our clients and their loved ones were able to continue growing and enjoying their new intimacy and connections down the road.

SUGGESTED RESOURCES and CONTACT INFORMATION

> **If you are in search of a loved one, here are the resources Troy has developed for your use or suggests:**

To Start Your Own Search Or To Be Considered For "The Locator" TV Show: www.TroyTheLocator.com

To Register On Troy's FREE Registry Where Reunions Happen Every Day, Go To: www.TroysList.ORG (Not .com!)

To Follow Troy's Blog And See Clips From *The Locator*, Go To: www.WeTV.com/TheLocator

You Can Also Follow Troy on Twitter! www.Twitter.com/TheLocator

See Tons Of Personal Family Videos and Stuff on his Facebook Page!   www.Facebook.com/TroyTheLocator

If your organization would like to book Troy as a speaker or have Troy's Leadership team provide your company with exciting training, contact:
Tami Spencer: tamispencer@artlover.com

About the Author

Troy Dunn is a successful entrepreneur with a focus on family values. Having grown up in a family touched by adoption, Troy saw a need for a service that facilitated the rebuilding of fractured families and those separated through various circumstances. Twenty years later, he and his team of passionate searchers and facilitators (led by his mother, Katie) have reunited tens of thousands of families around the world. He continues this life work today via WE tv's hit tv show, "*The Locator*".

In addition to his hit tv show, Troy is also the co-founder of Dunn–Hoisington Leadership International, LLC, an organization dedicated to teaching and developing leadership skills to Fortune 100 companies around the world. Troy is also seen frequently as a favorite business contributor on Fox News and CNBC.

As much as he enjoys his time rebuilding families or enhancing leadership in organizations, it all comes second behind his highest priority, his family.

Acknowledgements

A very special thanks to:

* VK, the one with the original vision for a locating organization and the man who helped me help Mom. * Dad, for teaching me to dream and dream BIG! * Mom, for signing on from day one and riding this crazy journey by my side. You made it all worth it. ILYFILYFA! * Roger, who saved us when we were drowning. * Suz & Lane, for your years of loyalty. * Jan B, my gifted writing partner who converts my rambling thoughts into the books which bear my name. * Kelly, who saw the potential of our show before any of us. * Ted H, the brilliant story teller who pioneered "The Locator". * Kim and the other amazing folks at WE tv who helped me take my personal mission to the world. * Steve & Jonathan at Asylum Entertainment for giving me the greatest, most compassionate production team in television history. (I LOVE YOU GUYS!) * TJ H, my friend, mindset mentor & business partner. Dude, you are an answer to a prayer. * The tens of thousands of people around the world who have trusted in me enough to share their hopes, fears and dreams with me along the journey to their own personal "peace". You lift me, teach me and you are proof the world is a better place than some might think. * Birthmothers everywhere. Thank you for making the selfless, courageous choice to give life.
* Lastly, most importantly, my Lord and Savior, Jesus Christ.

And in case I don't say it enough... Jen I LOVE YOU! NMW! :-)

More of the INSPIRATION you have been looking for—

If You Think You Can! *by TJ Hoisington*

If you want to achieve something, or get somewhere in life, you must understand the governing laws that turn dreams into reality. TJ shows you what habits must be formed and what steps must be taken to achieve any goal you set. Simple and concise, *If You Think You Can! 13 Laws the Govern the Performance of High Achievers* is a powerful source of inspiration that will help you achieve whatever you want.

What Are You Worth? *by Natalyn O. Lewis*

In this book, you will be taken on an emotional journey in pursuit of discovering your maximum potential. Through personal stories and well known illustrations, you will come to see that you are incredibly valuable and that you have the power to bring out the value in others as well.

Young Bucks *by Troy Dunn*

Young Bucks: *How to Raise a Future Millionaire* is on the cusp of an important new way of understanding how we earn, keep, and spend money. A self-made millionaire and father of seven, Troy Dunn gives you practical templates for easy, kid-friendly businesses that you can introduce to your children so that they can start earning their own money quickly.

To order visit **Amazon.com** or
www.AylesburyPublishing.com